Backward Glances

Backward Glances

Cruising the Queer Streets of New York and London

Mark W. Turner

REAKTION BOOKS

Published by Reaktion Books Ltd.
79 Farringdon Road
London EC1M 3JU, UK
www.reaktionbooks.co.uk

Printed and bound by Biddles Ltd, Guildford and King's Lynn

British Library Cataloguing in Publication Data

Turner, Mark W.
    Backward glances: cruising the queer streets of New York and
    London
    1.Homosexuality – England – London – History 2.Homosexuality – New
    York (State) – New York – History 3.Street life – England – London –
    History 4.Street life – New York (State) – New York – History 5.Subculture –
    England – London – History 6.Subculture – New York (State) – New York –
    History
    I.Title
    306.7'662'09421

ISBN 1 86189 180 6

Contents

Preface

This book begins in the late nineteenth century, and considers the ways different men moved through the streets of London and New York, making contact with other men. It was in the final decades of the nineteenth century that cruising got imagined (whether consciously or not) as a way of experiencing the modern city. This is not to say that men didn't meet men in the city before the late nineteenth century, before the full effects of the massive social and material changes wrought by urbanization and what we broadly call the industrial revolution. On the contrary, men have always made contact with other men in the city. However, cruising as I am discussing it emerges as a counter-discourse in the literature of modernity and an alternative street practice in the modern city, a way of both imagining and inhabiting the spaces of the city that challenge other ways we have come to understand urban movement, in particular through the overdetermining figure of the *flâneur*. Indeed, the cruiser rubs up against the *flâneur* frequently in this book, in part because the cruiser has, I think, for too long made invisible other kinds of street walking that suggest other interactions in urban modernity. Cruising is not presented here as a 'theory' that is explicitly articulated by anyone in particular, rather as one way of conceptualizing the man on the streets that exploits the ambivalences and uncertainties inherent in the city and in depictions of the city. The first chapter suggests that one of the primary ways that artists and writers in the mid- to late-nineteenth century imagined the city was through indeterminacy and fragmentation, and the gaps and uncertainties created by this vision

7

of modernity opened up a space, both real and conceptual, for the cruiser to inhabit. Largely, then, this is a book about representation and the ways writers and others have found to imagine the ambiguous meanings of a backward glance, rather than what we might call, rather strictly, urban or social history. But what I hope to emphasize throughout are the ways representation and 'real lives' impact upon one another, in and across history, in not always simplistic one-to-one ways. Fact and fiction blur here, as they always are wont to do, and much of the material I discuss requires us, at the very least, to interrogate our definitions of 'evidence' when it comes to marginalized, often hidden, urban practices from the past.

This book started out in my mind as something like a sweeping cultural history of cruising, but I abandoned that idea for a number of reasons. Chief among them, I increasingly felt that writing a macro 'history of' was simply not the correct approach. It suggested something too linear and too overarching that I am still not convinced is appropriate when thinking about cruising. What interests me about men looking at other men on the streets of modernity (or making contact with them, or encountering them – all these are ways of thinking about what cruising *is*) is the uncertainty of it all – the difficulty we now have in locating them, in recognizing them, in seeing them in our own backward glance at the past. In other words, when I first thought about this project, I thought it would do simply to write the history of certain cruisers, to name the places where men might have cruised, to provide a map of London and New York that reconsidered the streets from the cruisers' point of view. I wanted to connect my queer present to a knowable and certain queer past. But the project became more complicated because the ways and the reasons we use the past in order to think about the present are never simple to determine. While, on the one hand, I hope to shed some light on the past, it is not simply for its own sake and neither is it to provide an historical 'cruising continuum' to the present. Rather, I look to the past to help me understand something about cruising, and our cities, and sexuality, and the ways we have of representing all of these, in the present, *now*.

As I interpret it, cruising is the moment of visual exchange that occurs on the streets and in other places in the city, which constitutes an act of mutual recognition amid the otherwise alienating effects of the anonymous crowd. It is a practice that exploits the fluidity and multiplicity of the modern city to its advantage. But cruising is not transhistorical – like everything else, it is circumscribed by any number of social determinants and cultural and social specificities. And cruising is always site-specific. While I discuss certain kinds of practices and ways of being in the city that overlap, I am less interested in arriving at a single or singular way of understanding cruising than in considering the ways that cruising necessarily resists totalizing ways and is imagined as a process of counter-movement. This is one reason why this book is limited to men. Initially, I intended to write about women cruising as well, and I began to read and write about women in New York in the 1950s, and the ways cruising was imagined in the pulp fiction of queer women such as Ann Bannon. Her Beebo Brinker novels, for example, offer a wealth of material about the ways women took to the streets in the city, the ways they both responded to and reconfigured men's urban movement, and about raids on bars and the general tenuousness of queer culture for many women in New York in the mid-twentieth century. Bannon cleverly both borrows from and appropriates the tropes of male walking for her queer women and does so in ways that challenge our gendered assumptions about the streets and urban spaces generally. Her pulp fiction, like many others', is one place we can go to find out about the streets. After thinking about the different ways that men and women cruise I became convinced that women's cruising is its own important and distinct story. Indeed, cruising as a street practice needs to be far more fully considered in relation not only to issues of gender but also to race and ethnicity. While I focus on the connections between some mostly middle-class white men from the late nineteenth century to the late twentieth century – some well-known, others not at all – and try to suggest that even the movements of men who, arguably, were the most privileged walkers on the streets of modernity have been constrained by the ways we have of imagining them, I am keenly aware that this is not the whole story of cruising. There were other kinds of men walking, other ways of interacting on the streets, that point to equally significant forms of social contact. Too much writing about the city of modernity assumes that the ways we have of understanding the streets and its inhabitants are categorical. I believe, however, that examining more closely our assumptions about the street walking men of modernity may lead us to question other assumptions we have — about gender, about race and ethnicity, for example.

One of the questions that I return to throughout this book is a fairly simple one: how do we know a cruiser when we see him in the modern city? It can be a difficult enough question to consider even today, when 'cruising' or 'cottaging' are terms that many non-cruisers understand — given the representations of cruisers in the media, in our literature and in our popular culture generally. In its way, cruising is very much with us. Through such cult television programmes as *This Life* in the UK, in which a young lawyer named Warren gets arrested in a park toilet late at night, and *Queer as Folk* (both in the UK and its remake in the USA), in which promiscuity is taken for granted in gay male culture, the idea of cruising in the city and of multiple encounters has become well known. But what about late nineteenth-century culture, when queer appropriations of urban space also occurred, but were not represented in quite the same ways? In other words, where do we go for our sources when we wish to locate and think about cruising? There are a number of difficulties.

Not least, cruising is the stuff of fleeting, ephemeral moments not intended to be captured. The problem with writing about cruising is that of writing about many other urban experiences — it doesn't remain static, it passes quickly, it's over in the time it takes to shift one's eyes. But there *are* sources that capture such fleeting moments — Walt Whitman's notebooks are one that I discuss at length, but novels and other fiction equally offer us moments when a backward glance seems to suggest a moment of reciprocity on the streets. Journalism is arguably *the* literature of urban modernity in the sense that it exists as ephemera, superseded daily by the new, always becoming obsolete and forever impermanent. But we learn a great deal about our cities through the press, which continually shape and reshape geographies of crime, of sexual licence, of entertainment and pleasure for its readers. Certainly, in the twentieth century, one of the ways that cruising has been located is through arrests and prosecutions covered by the press. Men (particularly famous men, whether John Gielgud in London or George Michael in LA, but also hoards of unknown others – fathers, sons, brothers, uncles, friends) getting arrested in public toilets have provided material for historians who have been able to map in detail the sexual geographies of queer men. The mapping of sexual encounters in relation to urinal culture has been one of the ways the cruiser's city has been understood in the twentieth century. Personal diaries have also pointed to particular streets and other urban locales where cruising men gathered. But what is so remarkable about New York and London in the late nineteenth century is the lack of this type of material. The press frequently published accounts of men being arrested for indecent behaviour to men, women and children, but the exact nature of the actions is never made clear and, most often, the cases disappear from public view very quickly. We are frequently left with more questions than answers, as I suggest in chapters two and three. With the exception of such widely covered trials in London as that of the cross-dressers Boulton and Park in 1870 (which revealed the sexual fluidity of the West End theatre district), or the Cleveland Street scandal in 1889 (which located very specifically a male brothel), or the Wilde trials (which widely publicized queer urban practices of various sorts) – the routine, everyday lives of queer men cruising on the streets was not the stuff of popular reading. And because laws were different in the late nineteenth century in New York and London, it is even more difficult to locate a cruising geography through arrests and court documents.

The range of sources I discuss includes poetry, journalism, fiction, pornography, photography, autobiography, letters, journals and painting. Earl Lind's *Autobiography of an Androgyne* (1918) tells us a great deal about the significance of the Bowery or the 14th Street district for cruising in Manhattan in the 1890s, while Whitman's poetry teaches us about the radical impulse of cruising as a kind of ideal urban contact. A short story may have as much to tell us about the codes of cruising as an entry in a notebook that records a street encounter. I don't trust journalism any more than fiction, and don't believe that a photograph is any more accurate in its depiction of a street than a poem – all are part of the interrelated cultural production of the city and provide possibilities for understanding how cruising was imagined and how it gets reimagined over time. All this different kind of material offers us cruising traces that, if taken collectively and accumulatively, as they are here, reveal not only something about cruising in the modern city but also something about the fragmented, piecemeal shape that recording urban experiences can take.

In between the chapters are brief fragments of what could be other, more extended stories. Sometimes there are passing thoughts, and sometimes fragments linked to incidents in my own life. They are included as traces from a contemporary life that are (if only imaginatively) connected to other urban traces from the past. Each of these fragments suggests another trajectory that writing about cruising might take, another route with other lines of inquiry that the book could take. All of them suggest that understanding cruising today is enriched through an interaction with the past.

Let's suppose you are in a real city . . .

. . . and you are a man and you are walking down the street, in the thick of the crowd. Glancing up from the pavement, for just a moment, you notice a man walking in your direction and he's staring straight at you. Not every man fixes his stare before his feet at this violet hour, it seems. You don't. His stare hits you right between your eyes. And not for the first time. You recognize him. He has looked at you in this way before – and he has seen you see him do this before. Let's say he is about your age (whatever age that is) and he is wearing a suit, like you. You two could be twins, in the dark.

You don't know why, or rather, you don't at this particular moment ask yourself why, but you hold the gaze of this man who is now walking closer to you and who refuses not to look. Seconds pass, perhaps as many as five or six, but it seems like longer. Time slows down for you, as it always does in situations like these. In an instant, the gaze between you two is broken – you look down, or perhaps he looks away. Maybe someone passes between you, or something else diverts your attention. It's noisy, with the sound of horns and motors, but it could be anything. As quickly as the moment came upon you, it is lost. Almost. You look back, behind you, and see that he, too, is looking back behind him.

Let's say the city where this particular encounter takes place is London, and you are hurrying across London Bridge, in order to catch a train because you have a family to go home to, a ready-made microwave meal awaits, probably kids, the lot. You don't want to be late, not again, not again this week anyway. You look forward to your train journey, because this is your time, your very own time, the time between two lives, someone might say.

On the train home, settled into your seat, and for reasons you cannot explain to yourself or for reasons you really don't understand, the man on the street – your man on the street, handsome with a nice suit – comes back into your mind. He was never very far out of your mind, if truth be told. You are going a little red in the cheeks at the thought of it, even now. Did you go red in the cheeks when he was looking at you? Was it the blush of shame or the blush of desire? Do you know the difference between shame and desire? These are questions you could ask yourself, but don't.

Instead, you wonder if one day this man will speak to you. Speak to me, you think. Why do you never speak. What are you thinking? I never know what you are thinking.

Chapter One

Ambiguous Cities

Fragments of Modernity

In mid-nineteenth-century Paris, a man walks through the modern Carrousel adjacent to the Louvre. Old Paris is being transformed by Baron Haussmann, whose vision of new Paris creates wider streets, razes old buildings and displaces inhabitants. For the man walking through this site of urban regeneration, at least for a brief moment, the city 'more quickly shifts, alas, than does the moral heart' and the urban landscape of Paris, like the street walker's mind, is a vision of 'jumbled bric-à-brac'. Experiencing the city as and in flux, his mind takes on the attributes of the built environment — or the one impresses itself upon the other. It is a moment of clutter and collision, the result of history and memory erupting in the present as the streets of the romanticized past give way to the new and improved Paris. But it is also a moment of accumulation, in which the experiences and details of everyday life that constitute what it means to be modern in a transforming urban world are felt. The man's walk through Haussmann's Paris-to-be reveals the tension between an emerging city and a falling one, and produces a melancholic meditation on loss and the ability of memory to solidify experience and make meaning in the face of a modernizing city. By walking through the shifting urban landscape, the man's memory and desire collapse and are revealed to be part of one contemporaneous moment, in which the recollection of the past points to the future.[1]

This man, the speaker in Baudelaire's poem 'The Swan',[2] is one of the most well-known figures in the literature of urban modernity. Poems such as 'The Swan' from the *Tableaux parisiens* section of *Fleurs du Mal*, together with the prose poems in *Spleen de Paris* and a few seminal essays, have articulated a vision of the city that has become the dominant model for how we understand modernity. So much so that it is now a critical commonplace to link the two, as Baudelaire's influence on generations of later urbanists – surrealist painters, modernist writers, surreally modern philosophers – confirms. According to Marshall Berman, who has written so eloquently about modernity, Baudelaire was 'a prophet and a pioneer', 'a first modernist', who understood what it meant to live in the grip of the urban world.[3]

In another of Baudelaire's almost nightmarish visions of the modern city, Paris is imagined as a

> City of swarming, city full of dreams
> Where ghosts in daylight tug the stroller's sleeve!
> Mysteries everywhere run like the sap
> That fills this great colossus' conduits.

Swarming and haunted, the city is the stage for a ghoulish promenade of 'Seven Old Men', a 'parade from Hell'. The first old man to appear is a broken, divided one –

> You would not call him bent, but cut in two –
> His spine made a right angle with his legs
> So neatly that his cane, the final touch,
> Gave him the figure and the clumsy step

> Of some sick beast, or a three-legged Jew.
> In snow and filth he made his heavy way,
> As if his old shoes trampled on the dead
> In hatred, not indifference to life.[4]

He doubles, and then doubles again, and the appearance of each successive ragged old man suggests a never-ending, eternal 'conspiracy' of 'wicked chance'. Seven times the 'sinister old man' appears, leading to the speaker's 'frenetic state'. Is this an allegory of the poet's own alienation and mortality? Are the seven spectres versions of the same broken self? As if in anticipation of the broken-backed bodies of cubist representation, the figures here are fractured and multiplied, inhuman and in pieces. The individual breaks down into parts of the self, but also of others, so that fragmentation and brokenness are as much a part of Baudelaire's fraught modern urban condition as the frenetic state it creates and leaves behind.

The city is no kinder to 'The Little Old Women', whose bodies are also warped and fragmented. 'Dislocated wrecks' who 'toddle, every bit like marionettes' creep along the streets with broken bodies:

> Unless geometry occurs to me
> In shapes of these contorted limbs, and I
> Think how the workmen have to modify
> The boxes where these bodies will be lain.

They 'trudge on, stoic, without complaint,/Through the chaotic city's teeming waste', all the while under the watchful, even sympathetic eye of the speaker-voyeur who alone understands the beauty of the female ruins:

> I see your novice passions blossoming;
> Sombre or sunny, I see your lost days;
> Heart multiplied, I share in all your vice!
> With all your virtue shines my glowing soul!
>
> Ruins! my family! my fellow-minds![5]

Baudelaire's city is a vision of ruins; his Paris and its citizens require piecing together. Individual subjects who walk the city streets are fractured and warped and exist in a landscape of hostile dissembling. Yet it is precisely the bric-à-brac of modern city life that offers the urban poet the opportunity to reassemble and to recreate – to locate through the imagination and the workings of memory a way of bringing together the fragments of the modernity.

Although Baudelaire imagines the Hausmannization of Paris with its shifting neighbourhoods, open boulevards and new kinds of buildings and architecture as a phantasmagoric dreamscape, the city of fragments was a real, material fact in the redevelopment of Paris. To be modern and to be urban (and to be the one is to be the other) is, in part, to experience the shock of that fragmentation. What it means to walk the streets in Baudelaire's Paris is to confront multitudinous stimuli in a rush of different and competing images, but it also allows the privileged poet and artist a dreamworld of the imagination, which breaks down barriers between private and public, self and other in captured *tableaux*. As he tells us in his prose poem 'The Crowds',

> The poet benefits from an incomparable privilege which allows him to be, at will, himself and others. Like those wandering souls in search of a body, he enters, when he so desires, into the character of each individual. For him alone, everything is vacant; and if certain places appear to be closed to him, that is because in his eyes they are not worth the bother of visiting.
>
> The solitary and pensive stroller finds this universal communion extraordinarily intoxicating.[6]

The speaker who confronts the seven grisly old men and contorted old whores becomes those men and women; he merges imaginatively with their lives and a kind of perverse connection is made, in which the solitary stranger and the crowd are one and the same. This is what it means to 'plunge into the multitude'. This is what he calls the 'art to enjoying the crowd'.

Baudelaire conceptualizes this art form most fully in his often cited article of 1863, 'The Painter of Modern Life', in which he describes the quintessential modern man, 'the hero of modern life', in the figure of that painter of everyday life, Constantin Guys:

> The crowd is his domain, just as the air is the bird's, and the water that of the fish. His passion and his profession is to merge with the crowd. For the perfect idler, for the passionate observer it becomes an immense source of enjoyment to establish his dwelling in the throng, in the ebb and flow, the bustle, the fleeting and the infinite.[7]

What the modern man does in the shapeshifting crowd is walk, and he keeps walking as if in search of something, as if to maximize his chances for stumbling upon something, but something imprecise:

> And so, walking or quickening his pace, he goes his way, for ever in search. In search of what? We may rest assured that this man, such as I have described him, this solitary mortal endowed with an active imagination, always roaming the great desert of men, has a nobler aim than that of the pure idler, a more general aim, other than the fleeting pleasure of circumstance. He is looking for that indefinable something we may be allowed to call 'modernity', for want of a better term to express the idea in question. The aim for him is to extract from fashion the poetry that resides in its historical envelope, to distil the eternal from the transitory.[8]

Later, in a phrase that will come to define the experience of being modern for many, Baudelaire announces that: 'Modernity is the transient, the fleeting, the contingent; it is one half of art, the other being the eternal and the immovable.'[9]

Baudelaire's definition sets up an ongoing tension between the ephemeral and the permanent, a conflict that is one of the productive features of modernity,[10] but he was not alone in trying to conceptualize the peculiar ambiguities, aesthetic and otherwise, of the emerging urban world. If Baudelaire was the prophet, as Berman puts it, then others were quick to follow. Many others – some his contemporaries, others in the generation after him – took as their subject the transience of contemporary life and/or the contingent nature of life in the city. Poets such as Walt Whitman in New York and James Thomson, John Davidson, Ernest Dowson and Amy Levy in London; novelists including Dickens and Gaskell, Zola and Gissing; painters such as Monet and Pissarro; photographers like Atget; and any number of urban sketch journalists, all found in the 'indefinable something' of urban experience a certain something that was particularly and peculiarly modern, something like a modern aesthetic that needed to be explored through representation. All went in search of the modern city and found a form of uncertainty.

Like Baudelaire, James McNeill Whistler was one of those who argued eloquently for a vision of the city that captured the ambivalences of everyday life, its ambiguities and its dissolution. His was an aesthetic of the contingent. Nowhere is this more poetically articulated than in his 'Ten O'Clock Lecture', which attacks realist modes of representation because 'to say to the painter, that Nature is to be taken as she is, is to say to the player, that he may sit on the piano'.[11] Far from following the dictates of Nature, the modern artist should embrace the tentative and the indeterminate, qualities that are nowhere more powerfully a part of everyday life than in the city:

And when the evening mist clothes the riverside with poetry, as with a veil, and the poor buildings lose themselves in the dim sky, and the tall chimneys become campanili, and the warehouses are palaces in the night, and the whole city hangs in the heavens, and fairy-land is before us – then the wayfarer hastens home; the working man and the cultured one, the wise man and the one of pleasure, cease to understand, as they have ceased to see, and Nature, who, for once, has sung in tune, sings her exquisite song to the artist alone, her son and her master – her son in that he loves her, her master in that he knows her.[12]

As the mist moves casting an uncertain pall, the city becomes a place of poetry, released from the precision (and harsh light) of day into the unfolding ambiguity of evening. For Whistler, London is a place of enchantment, its industrial smokestacks transformed into a romantic vision of Renaissance towers. Moments of transition when one thing becomes another as time passes hint at a city that is almost illusory. His fondness for twilight in the city was part of his modern tendency and provides a link with contemporaneous urban visionaries.[13] Both Whistler and Baudelaire loved the dusk and dawn and were bewitched by those moments of alteration in the city when the light plays tricks and when the streets are at their most uncertain and confounding. In Baudelaire's 'Dusk', as 'Sweet evening comes' daytime workers head home, night-time wanderers (criminals, robbers, prostitutes and other 'corrupting demons') take to the streets, but daytime and night-time creatures rub shoulders and occupy the same space. All overlap. This is the time Baudelaire elsewhere calls 'the witching hour, the uncertain light, when the sky draws its curtains and the city lights go on'.[14] It is no surprise, then, that Baudelaire was an admirer of Whistler. Although he did not live to see many of Whistler's greatest paintings from the 1870s, Baudelaire wrote appreciably about his Thames engravings shown in Paris in 1862, proclaiming that they were as 'subtle, as alert as improvisation and inspiration, representing the banks of the Thames; a wonderful jumble of rigging, yardarms, ropes; a chaotic amalgam of fog, furnaces, and corkscrew fumes; the profound and complex poetry of a vast city'.[15]

Baudelaire's 'uncertain light' is similar to that found in Whistler's *Nocturne* series, which celebrate, perhaps more effectively than any other paintings in the late nineteenth century, the poetic beauty of urban ambiguity. Like other Impressionists who captured the transience of light in the city – most obviously Monet in his paintings of London and Paris – Whistler tries to transform an essentially ephemeral experience into something permanent and, in so doing, produces images that we can read as displacements of time and of space on the canvas. Like Baudelaire's poems, Whistler's city seems to exist outside real time, even as it seeks to capture the mood, atmosphere and tone of a particular moment in time. Consider the *Nocturne in Blue and Gold: Old Battersea Bridge* (1872–5) which is wholly unconcerned with the realistic depiction of the river as evening comes; instead, it is a canvas with a mood of uncertainty – where do particular figures begin and end, what are the shapes and contours on the bridge – that reveals, through harmony rather than Baudelairean rupture, something about the city and the approaching night. But, like Baudelaire, Whistler's city of dissolving and disappearing colours and forms was a city of reconfiguration through memory. Whistler did not usually paint from nature when producing the *Nocturnes*; on the contrary he went boating on the Thames and walked through the city making sketches of particular moments and scenes which he would use as the basis for the paintings. The sketch would be reconfigured and transformed into something quite else through the act of memory.[16]

For both the poet and the painter, the city at twilight was a way of exciting the imagination through memory, a way of rewriting and reconfiguring – of representing rather than recording – the past in the present. Whistler's *Nocturnes* do not suggest the kind of fragmentation found in Baudelaire's bric-à-brac, and yet the lack of definition in Whistler's paintings, the murkiness of the greens and greys with flashes of colour here and there, suggest a similar sense of uncertainty and dislocation in the city. Whistler, too, evokes Baudelaire's city of 'mysteries everywhere'.

The more you look at the mid-nineteenth-century city of modernity, the more elusive and undefinable it becomes. Whistler's misty veil over the poetic Thames is not so far from Dickens's London, with its 'fog everywhere'. While for Whistler the impenetrable fog is part of the beauty and poetry of the urban aesthetic (it unites the landscape), for Dickens it suggests a far less harmonious city, in which the truth can never ultimately be known. Like Baudelaire's Paris, Dickens's London is a city of turmoil and fragments. Nowhere is this made so plain as in *Dombey and Son* (1848) in which the arrival of the railway is imagined as 'the first shock of a great earthquake' that reconfigures neighbourhoods such as Staggs's Gardens:

James McNeill Whistler, *Nocturne in Blue and Gold: Old Battersea Bridge*, 1872–5, oil on canvas. Tate Britain, London.

There was no such place as Staggs's Gardens. It had vanished from the earth. Where the old rotten summer-houses once had stood, palaces now reared their heads, and granite columns of gigantic girth opened a vista to the railway world beyond. The miserable waste ground, where the refuse-matter had been heaped of yore, was swallowed up and gone; and in its frowsy stead were tiers of warehouses, crammed with rich goods and costly merchandise. The old by-streets now swarmed with passengers and vehicles of every kind: the new streets that had stopped disheartened in the mud and waggon-ruts, formed towns within themselves, originating wholesome comforts and conveniences belonging to themselves, and never tried nor thought of until they sprung into existence. Bridges that had led to nothing, led to villas, gardens, churches, healthy public walks. The carcasses of houses, and beginnings of new thoroughfares, had started off upon the line at steam's own speed, and shot away into the country in a monster train.[17]

As in Baudelaire, there is a real social cost to the modernization (here caused by commercialization) of the city. Elsewhere, Dickens addresses modern uncertainty by trying to hold the city and its people together metaphorically; indeed, one of his great gifts in writing about the city was to create those images of urban modernity that could extend and stretch to accommodate the whole. He gives us the Circumlocution Office and Court of Chancery representing nightmarish entanglement in an increasingly institutionalized urban world without transparency. There is the great Dust Heap, an image of endless recycling but also of the commodification of detritus, shit and excess in the world's largest city. And, of course, there is the fog that everywhere prevents the truth from being easily known and the city from being easily seen; in the 'heavy and dark' fog of Our Mutual Friend (1865) 'the whole metropolis was a heap of vapour charged with muffled sound of wheels, and enfolding a gigantic catarrh'.[18] Throughout his works, perhaps especially in Bleak House, Dickens seeks to capture and contain the heaving, unruly and gothic metropolis through the grand gesture of metaphor on the one hand, and through the development of intricate social networks on the other, to suggest that we are all part of one massive, teeming, labyrinthine world of secrets in which the repressed always comes back to haunt us.

Yet, for all the power of his metaphors and the intricacies of his social worlds, the vision of London in a novel such as *Bleak House* does not quite cohere. In fact, in his attempt to metaphorize the experience of life in the metropolis, Dickens demonstrates the difficulty in trying to make a world that is experienced as fragmentation and dislocation cohere, even imaginatively. While Baudelaire sees in the uneven bric-à-brac nature of urban experience a way to make the transient permanent — indeed, to make it definitive of what it means to be modern — Dickens tries to unite the fragmented parts of modern life. There is an overstretching at times, almost an insistent yearning, to make the contemporary city understandable and decipherable. No surprise, then, that it is Dickens who introduces the first fictional detective into English literature, Inspector Buckett, to solve the mysteries everywhere in the midst of all that fog. It is the detective's job to bring together the fragments and disparate clues of the modern metropolis that will eventually solve the mysteries at the centre of the narrative. And still the novel reveals its seams throughout, most obviously in the use of two narrative voices to tell the story. Esther Summerson's autobiographical narrative (effectively a search for identity) competes with the detached omniscient narrator for the reader's attention, and they take turns trying to illuminate the mysteries of the city — one from inside, one detached and distant, both inside and outside the narrative. Whose story is most valid? Who should we believe? A single voice, it seems, will not do, at least not here — a single way of seeing and describing events needs to be countered or complemented by other ways of seeing and telling. No one story can tell all or reveal the 'truth' of this modern Babylon. This is not to suggest that because the novel does not cohere in this way, it is necessarily a failure. Far from it, *Bleak House* succeeds brilliantly in pushing us to see the city, as a subject and as a state of mind, as essentially fragmented, unknowable and open-ended.

Teasingly, *Bleak House* ends with an ambivalent sentence fragment. The final words are 'even supposing –', so the reader is left with an immediate and obvious question: even supposing what? Like so many Victorian novels, this one ends with marriage, which usually indicates social cohesion for the future. But beyond the social contract of marriage, there is uncertainty in the open-ended and indeterminate sentence fragment – a fragment that asks us to continue thinking about things and to project a future. This fragment may be the final words of this great London novel, but it is clearly not the end of the story, nor can it be. The disorder and ambiguity of the city may be made to cohere, however awkwardly at times, but not forever, because the natural state of urban modernity tends toward uncertainty, and Dickens felt that uncertainty. London was in flux every bit as much as Paris and the proof was all around him. As Lynda Nead suggests:

> This was the nature of London's modernity; it seemed to obey the spatial logic of the maze, rather than that of the grid or the *étoile*, and its characteristic experience was of disorientation, as opposed to purposeful movement. The modernization of London in the nineteenth century was partial and uneven. It was circumscribed by conflicting urban visions and created as much in relation to perceptions of the city's past as it was in terms of the formation of the new and in the interests of the future.[19]

Dickens does not set out to write what will end up being a formally ruptured novel, not in the way later modernist urban writers will (John Dos Passos, T. S. Eliot, Virginia Woolf, James Joyce and others). Rather the subject matter and focus on London inevitably leads Dickens, if not quite to T. S. Eliot's 'heap of broken images', then at least to the never-ending uncertainties thrown up by a disorienting city in which there is 'fog everywhere'.

To think of this another way, one approach to the shifting nature of urban modernity is to find ways of imposing order on it, while still allowing for the complexity of a city of multitudes, and Dickens's great metaphorical gestures do just that. So, too, the great urban 'cataloguers' of nineteenth-century cities – especially a figure like Henry Mayhew whose *London Labour and the London Poor* tries to locate and describe so many different urban 'types' – each in their way attempt to make the city knowable and so less anxiety-provoking by revealing its secrets. Social investigation – exploring the slums, in particular, and revealing them to the middle-class reader – becomes one of the most important genres of urban writing toward the end of the century, as the cities of modernity get larger and larger and seemingly less decipherable. Booth's *In Darkest London*, Mrs Bernard Bosanquet's *Rich and Poor*, Jacob Riis's *How the Other Half Lives* – just a few examples of the vast literature of investigation that sought in different ways to demystify the city, to make familiar that which had hitherto remained unglimpsed and so unknown.[20] Taken together, these attempts to describe all the kinds of difference the city contains end up, finally, suggesting that a complete, total picture of the city is really not possible. You cannot catalogue it all.

But you can try, as does Walt Whitman in New York. He embraced the crowd like few others and took on the burden of representing the multitude; indeed, for Whitman, he and the multitude are as one – 'Walt Whitman, a kosmos, of Manhattan the son', he writes in 'Song of Myself'. In this long poem, far from being an alienating experience, the multitude of the urban masses represents a communing with others that is an overwhelmingly positive feature of contemporary life:

This is the city and I am one of the citizens,
Whatever interests the rest interests me, politics, wars, markets, newspapers, schools,
The mayor and councils, banks, tariffs, steamships, factories, stocks, stores, real estate and personal estate.
The little plentiful manikins skipping around in collars and tail'd coats,
I am aware who they are, (they are positively not worms or fleas,)

I acknowledge the duplicates of myself, the weakest and
   shallowest is deathless with me,
What I do and say the same waits for them,
Every thought that flounders in me the same flounders in
   them.[21]

As he says more simply earlier in the poem, 'I will not have a
single person slighted or left away'. The openness and
inclusiveness of Whitman's poems and the freedom that he
endlessly advocates is what I take to be as a celebration of
fragments; for him, recognizing the multitude was part of
America's particular democratic project, which finds an ideal
manifestation in the city. As I will suggest in another chapter, the
many different kinds of experience on the streets of the city
explored by Whitman open up an interpretive space for
alternative readings of the social encounters in the city that exploit
the very fragmented fleetingness of modernity.

The Man on the Street

Baudelaire experiences the ambiguities of the city's fragmented
and uncertain moments by walking and watching, in the role of
the *flâneur*, he who enjoys the art of the crowd, who relishes the
fleeting, ephemeral moments of everyday urban life:

And he watches the flow of life move by, majestic and dazzling.
He admires the eternal beauty and the astonishing harmony of
life in the capital cities, a harmony so providentially maintained
in the tumult of human liberty. He gazes at the landscape of the
great city, landscapes of stone, now swathed in the mist, now
struck in full face by the sun. He enjoys handsome equipages,
proud horses, the spit and polish of the grooms, the skilful
handling by the page boys, the smooth rhythmical gait of the
women, the beauty of the children, full of the joy of life and
proud as peacocks of their pretty clothes; in short, life
universal.[22]

The hero of modern life, the *flâneur* consumes each passing moment – his is a life of visual encounters, all the while maintaining a detached, anonymous and essentially distant relation to the urban landscape he moves through. He looks but is rarely seen. A seemingly passive stroller – his strolling suggests leisure, he leans in doorways, he observes from the windows of cafés – the *flâneur* is no less a compulsive. This is something Baudelaire learned from Edgar Allan Poe, whom Baudelaire greatly admired and whose works (and ideas) he translated into French. In Poe's 'The Man of the Crowd' (1840), a convalescing urban man delights in 'scrutinizing the mob' and creating a typology of urban classes as night draws in:

> As the night deepened, so deepened to me the interest of the scene; for not only did the general character of the crowd materially alter (its general features retiring in the gradual withdrawal of the more orderly portion of the people, and its harsher ones coming out into bolder relief, as the late hour brought forth every species of infamy from its den), but the rays of the gas-lamps, feeble at first in their struggle with the dying day, had now at length gained ascendancy, and there over every thing a fitful and garish luster.[23]

Under the influence of the 'wild effects of the light', the narrator fixes his observational gaze on one man whom he follows in the streets of the city all night and into morning, in a compulsive and seemingly endless pursuit of the crowd. It is this compulsive quality – an almost helpless and even desperate need always to be not only *in* but also *of* the crowd – that has made him such a compelling figure in the modern imagination.

Walter Benjamin has done more than anyone else in extending Baudelaire's *flâneur* as the Ur-man of urban modernity, although he does this in at times particularly ambiguous ways. For Benjamin, this urban wanderer is a figure whose fluid movements in the city break down the division between private space and public space, so that 'the street becomes a dwelling for the *flâneur,* he is as much at home among the facades of houses as a citizen is in his four walls'.[24] The city and the crowd provide endless mysteries, and the stroller, like Poe's 'man of the crowd', becomes, in effect, a kind of 'unwilling detective', behind whose seemingly idle indolence is 'the watchfulness of an observer who does not take his eyes off a miscreant'.[25] But by abandoning himself in the crowd, maintaining an anonymous distance from others, voyeuristically objectifying the world around him, the *flâneur*, Benjamin argues, in turn becomes objectified or commodified, in turn becomes that which he so compulsively follows:

> The *flâneur* is someone abandoned in the crowd. In this he shares the situation of the commodity. He is not aware of the special situation, but this does not diminish its effect on him and it permeates him blissfully like a narcotic that can compensate him for many humiliations. The intoxication to which the *flâneur* surrenders is the intoxication of the commodity around which surges the stream of customers.[26]

As Benjamin reads him, Baudelaire's *flâneur* enacts the commodification of the individual that Marx suggested was a result of urban modernity. Readings of Benjamin that emphasize the totalizing aspects of the *flâneur* have often dominated discussions of Baudelaire and of urban modernity generally. Indeed, they have overdetermined how we read Baudelaire and how we interpret the city. So ubiquitous is this hero of modern life that hardly a man walking down a street in a Western city is thought of as anything other than a *flâneur*. Latter-day versions of the *flâneur* can be found in such representations as the *film noir* detective searching the streets (from Philip Marlowe to *Blade Runner*), but also the criminal who moves about unnoticed (think Alain Delon's assassin in Jean-Pierre Melville's *Le Samouraï*). Equally, he appears reconfigured as the estranged, existential modern man, in a perpetual state of alienation – an underground man updated in such figures as Sartre's anti-heroes and the loner Travis prowling the streets of New York in Scorsese's *Taxi Driver*.

And yet the idea of the *flâneur* has not gone unchallenged. As greater attention was paid to issues such as gender and sexuality in the city, in the wake of feminism in the 1960s and '70s, very simple questions were asked: where was the woman of the crowd? Did she exist and, if so, did she inhabit the same streets with the same anonymous pose? Of course, others walked and others were a part of the crowd, but the point is that not everyone inhabits the streets the same, or equally.

Feminist critics of art and literature have, in particular, pointed to the limitations of Benjamin's critique of the modern, by noting that *flânerie* is a gendered practice. Most notably, Janet Wolff in an important essay from 1985 argues that those defining urban figures, 'the dandy, the *flâneur*, the hero, the stranger – all figures invoked to epitomise the experience of modern life – are invariably male figures'.[27] She suggests that because the modern city is portrayed and theorized as an essentially male domain, there is no place for women, no space in the street for a female stroller, a *flâneuse*.[28] Deborah Epstein Nord challenges the dominance of men in the streets by arguing that 'the particular urban vision of the female observer, novelist, or investigator derives from her consciousness of transgression and trespassing, from the vexed sexuality her position implies, and from her struggle to escape the status of spectacle and become a spectator'.[29] In other words, women had their own ways of inhabiting the streets, their own ways of seeing. Other critics have discussed the presence of women in the streets by arguing that the urban female stroller can be seen in such figures as the window shopper, for example – a woman who walks the streets leisurely taking in visual pleasures.[30] Or, there is Sally Munt's study of lesbian identity and cultural space which appropriates the category of the *flâneur* for marginalized identities.[31] She reads the *flâneur* metaphorically, and notes the importance of freedom of movement and urban pleasure – defining qualities of the *flâneur* – in lesbian literature throughout the twentieth century. Rather than replace the category, Munt takes it over and in so doing reconfigures it. Both Wolff and Munt in their different ways seek to open up the critical category of the *flâneur* and allow for alternate ways of understanding urban movement, which usefully creates space for many kinds of street walkers.

New interpretations of the *flâneur* have varied, but not all have been as radical in their implications as some of those mentioned above. In a recent study of representations of London in the first half of the nineteenth century, Dana Arnold adopts the line that the male *flâneur* had a counterpart in the female *flâneuse* and that more or less all of the emerging metropolitan *bourgeoisie* were either one or the other:

> The emergence of a new bourgeois metropolitan personality which found expression in the architecture and street life of London – especially the West End – means the concept of the flaneur/euse is an effective way of examining the social and cultural modernity of the metropolis. Male and female experience of the London streets did differ, however. The flaneur or anonymous male viewer had greater freedom to roam the streets and visit the clubs and other places of public entertainment and edification which proliferated in this period . . . The increasing appearance of 'respectable' women in public spaces, albeit heavily chaperoned, meant there was a flaneuse in early nineteenth-century London and she visited and was seen in public parks, shopping arcades and garden squares.[32]

Arnold is keen to hold in place the conceptual framework of *flânerie*, but in order to do this, extends the privilege to women in the city in a fairly uncomplicated way. So instead of the *flâneur* being a category that describes the bourgeois metropolitan man, it is a category that can extend to the bourgeois woman as well, in a new kind of metropolitan centre. Arnold attempts to get round the overarching tendency of the concept of the *flâneur* by suggesting that women were out on the streets, too. There is a conceptual difficulty in an approach that simply extends *flânerie* and uses its practices as a way of describing the bourgeoisie: not *all* bourgeois men were *flâneurs*; not all bourgeois men inhabit the city and walk the streets in the same phantasmagorical way all the time. There is no allowing for different kinds of bourgeois men's experiences, different either from other men or from bourgeois women. Arnold repeats — indeed, falls into the trap of — others for whom *flânerie* serves as a theoretical framework that explains all ways of being/seeing in the streets of modernity without sufficient complexity in relation to such social determinants as gender.

While Baudelaire's street walker remains prominent in discussions of the city, his mastery of the streets has at least been questioned. Benjamin's reading of the *flâneur* has been shown to hide too much, to make too many assumptions and to be too insistent. Each of the critiques I have mentioned in passing above is an attempt to broaden the concept of *flânerie*, to make it more inclusive and less totalizing. But it may be helpful to return to Baudelaire, as Deborah Parsons does in her book on women in the modern city, *Streetwalking the Metropolis*. Parsons suggests that a multiple, shifting understanding of *flânerie* exists in Baudelaire all along; it simply depends on how we read his poetry.[33] Rather than being a totalizing, detached figure endlessly objectifying the city and its dwellers, Baudelaire's *flâneur* is a more fluid, more tentative figure. As Parsons puts it, 'the act of walking, as a body *within* the city, seems incompatible with the need to be a totalising, panoramic and authoritative viewpoint, of being the eye that *observes* it'.[34] In Baudelaire's 'To a Woman Passing By', she points out, there is a kind of reciprocal vision when the woman being objectified by the narrator's male gaze returns the look:

Around me roared the nearly deafening street.
Tall, slim, in mourning, in majestic grief,
A woman passed me, with a splendid hand
Lifting and swinging her festoon and hem;

Nimble and stately, statuesque of leg.
I, shaking like an addict, from her eye,
Black sky, spawner of hurricanes, drank in
Sweetness that fascinates, pleasure that kills.

One lightning flash . . . then night! Sweet fugitive
Whose glance has made me suddenly reborn,
Will we not meet again this side of death?

Far from this place! too late! *never* perhaps!
Neither one knowing where the other goes,
O you I might have loved, as well you know![35]

The passing woman, too, has agency; she, too, reads the street visually. It is not simply a case of objectification, though that is a part of the visual exchange; rather, there is a more complex interaction – of mutual looking, a kind of engagement in the moment of the glance. The point is that there *are* different ways of seeing in Baudelaire, other than the fixed gaze of the *flâneur*, which indicate a less rigid model of urban movement than we have tended to allow. This is significant because it acknowledges new possibilities for understanding what it means to walk and to look in the city of modernity. What is so helpful about Parsons's reading is that she returns us to ambiguous and uncertain modern streets, the streets, arguably, that we find in Whistler, Dickens, Whitman and so many others. The problem is the use of the category of the *flâneur*, which prevents us from seeing all the many ways there are of walking a street, all the many ways there are of seeing and being seen. All of the critiques I have mentioned leave intact an essentially binary grip (male/female) on our understanding of the city and urban movement. Even in the most provocative revisionist accounts of *flânerie*, the gendered terms *flâneur* and *flâneuse* fail to account for all the ways men and women might move through the city, creating different meanings in urban space; that is, the ways men might move different from other men, and women from other women.

The inability of the *flâneur*ial rule to apply to everyone, even to all bourgeoisie, is best illustrated by noting some of the exceptions. I have already mentioned women, but what about a bourgeois man who dresses as a woman – a cross-dresser, or a transvestite – how does he walk the streets, and how is he interpreted by others on the streets? He, too, was passing (in both senses of that word) in the streets of London and other capital cities. Or men who walked the streets – casually, leisurely – and, far from remaining detached like Poe's 'Man of the Crowd', actually met other men? In other words, what about the cruisers? *Flânerie* doesn't adequately account for all chance encounters. Far from it, it veils many of them; that is why it is necessary to think about ways of inhabiting the streets that resist the tendencies of the *flâneur*, and to find out who else may have been walking the streets of the city alongside him. There is a paradox in the way some have used the concept of *flânerie*. On the one hand, it has been extremely useful in helping us to understand ephemeral and fragmented experiences, while on the other offering us an overarching view of modernity that *explains* all the uncertainty of an urban world of fleeting moments. The city's passers-by, its loafers, its shoppers, its workers, its prostitutes, its cruisers – they all had their own way of moving and walking, of loitering with intent. All exist in a visual and spatial economy that is fundamentally uncertain and ambiguous, and this is why, for example, the middle-class window-shopping woman can be mistaken for a prostitute, as happened on occasion. This is also why the cruiser can be so easily mistaken for a *flâneur*. All had their own kinds of experiences – ephemeral, fleeting, lost.

We cannot pin down and define all men and all women in the streets because the city offers us much more ambiguous and contested spaces and places. The ways we understand the city have been revised in recent years, so that *place* – a geographical location – must be considered alongside ideas of *space* – how we inhabit and fill up an area or place. As Michel de Certeau puts it, 'space is practiced place. Thus the street geometrically defined by urban planning is transformed into a space by walkers.'[36] Meaning is determined by action, by what occurs on the streets. There is no singular, controlling 'eye' (or 'I') in the city, merely innumerable walkers, urban practitioners, 'whose bodies follow the thicks and thins of an urban "text" they write without being able to read it'.[37]

Each individual movement in the city constitutes its own poem, for Certeau, so in a city of infinite walkers, each inscribing his or her own text, the *flâneur* becomes only one of many possible ways of reading the street walker, only one stroller – and still arguably, a mostly male, heterosexual one – among others. The cruiser, I suggest, is one of the alternate ways of reading the urban street walker who exists in an environment of uncertain, ambiguous signification. Like every other street walker, the cruiser writes his own text of the city, but it may be a text not all of us can read equally. He is the anonymous wanderer who bathes in the multitude (*pace* Baudelaire) or botanizes on the asphalt (as Benjamin would have it) in order to seek out another individual – to find that other whose gaze will meet his own. The cruiser positively *longs* to be seen, but not by everyone, and not in all streets.

More suggestive in understanding the cruisers of urban modernity is Benjamin's great *Arcades Project*, only recently translated into English, which celebrates the idea of the fragment and allows for more arbitrary, random connections to be made in the city. The *Arcades Project* is Benjamin's unfinished (and perhaps unfinishable) masterwork, the culmination of his thinking about history and philosophy, modernity, commodification and capitalism, and the city. It is a difficult work to describe: at a very simple level it is a massive exercise in note-taking. Benjamin's technique is one of accumulation, of collection or, as the translators of the English edition describe it, an attempt to think about the fragments, rather than the unifying, overarching narratives of urban modernity:

> It was not the great men and celebrated events of traditional historiography but rather the 'refuse' and 'detritus' of history, the half-concealed, variegated traces of the daily life of 'the collective,' that was to be the object of study, and with the aid of methods more akin – above all, in their dependence on chance – to the methods of the nineteenth-century collector of antiquities and curiosities, or indeed to the methods of the

nineteenth-century ragpicker, than to those of the modern historian. Not conceptual analysis but something like dream interpretation was the model.[38]

Benjamin sat in the reading room at the Bibliothèque Nationale producing his myriad notes, a life's work that could never reach completion because of the very nature of the endeavour. Like the city itself, it was a project that could never pause. Arranged according to broad and diverse categories of investigation, Benjamin's 'Convolutes' – including such topics as 'Boredom'; 'Eternal Return'; 'Baudelaire'; 'The Flaneur'; 'The Streets of Paris'; 'Marx'; 'The Doll, The Automaton' – investigate the stuff of modern experience through cutting and pasting quotations from his extensive reading in the library and responding to them with his own observations and questions. It's like a vast catalogue of citation and commentary that we are meant to read dialectically, urging us toward greater understanding of the modern world. But the dialectic of modernity leaves us uncertain, as Benjamin remarks: 'Ambiguity is the manifest imaging of dialectic, the law of dialectics at a standstill.'[39] The ambiguity the reader feels in sifting through Benjamin's bundles of notes is like the ambiguity at the centre of modernity, expressed as an endless, ongoing dialectic. At first glance, the *Arcades Project* is seemingly random – like a stroll through the arcades, with its dreamlike display of objects and sights – but there are numerous routes through it, enabling each of us to wander through the text making our own way, mapping our own sets of connections and finding our own resonances by chance.

Benjamin learned a lot from Baudelaire, and the scene of 'jumbled bric-à-brac' in Baudelaire's 'The Swan' looks forward to the kinds of curious juxtapositions set up in the sections of the *Arcades Project*. Consider these notes from the section on Baudelaire:

In his poem 'L'Heautontimoroumenos' [The Self-Tormentor], Baudelaire himself speaks of his shrill voice.

A decisive value is to be accorded Baudelaire's efforts to capture the gaze in which the magic distance is extinguished. (Compare 'L'Amour du mensonge.') Relevant here: my definition of the aura as the aura of distance opened up with the look that awakens in an object perceived.

The gaze in which the magic of distance is extinguished: 'Let your eyes plunge into the fixed stare/of satyresses or water sprites' ('L'Aventisseur' [The Lookout]).[40]

Lines from Baudelaire, a comment on Baudelaire, a link to his own thinking – we see in the assemblage of diverse passages throughout the project the wandering mind, connecting like with unlike, idea with object, reflection with speculation, question with answer, this with that. By isolating lines from Baudelaire he reminds us of the poem, but also makes it less familiar. Benjamin moves from a comment on voice to comments on vision and spatial perspective, which he then connects and makes his own by introducing the notion of 'aura', discussed more formally and extensively elsewhere in his writing. It is fascinating to read through the Convolutes watching Benjamin's glances, his intellectual turns. But it is equally fascinating for the reader to wander through Benjamin's passages making his own connections, mapping his own way through the at times overwhelming abundance of material.

Here are a few passages from the section on 'The Flaneur':

Simmel's apt remark concerning the uneasiness aroused in the urbanite by other people, people whom, in the overwhelming majority of cases, he sees without hearing, would indicate that, at least in their beginnings, the physiognomies [correction: physiologies] were motivated by, among other things, the wish to dispel this uneasiness and render it harmless. Otherwise, the fantastic pretensions of these little volumes could not have sat well with their audience.

There is effort to master the new experiences of the city within the framework of the old traditional experiences of nature. Hence the schemata of the virgin forest and the sea (Meryon and Ponson du Terrail).

Trace and aura. The trace is appearance of nearness, however far removed from the thing that left it behind may be. The aura is appearance of a distance, however close the thing that calls it forth. In the trace, we gain possession of the thing; in the aura, it takes possession of us.[41]

In this glimpse, we move from Georg Simmel on nineteenth-century physiologies to Benjamin's own ideas on aura. Here, aura is contrasted with trace, and again, understanding each has to do with the urban gaze and how we see. It could, but doesn't have to, lead you back to the section on Baudelaire, as it did for me. That's one connection I make. But depending on how you navigate your way through the structure of this elaborate collection of fragments, you may end up somewhere else. It is uncertain and it communicates its ideas through chance encounters. The kinds of moves Benjamin makes throughout the *Arcades Project* work in precisely this way: we stumble, seemingly randomly, on an idea considered somewhere else (Benjamin's own traces?) with the effect of making things appear nearer. It puts things in dialogue in unexpected, unlooked-for ways.

In one way, the *Arcades Project* is an unrealized project that seeks to understand modernity through the accumulation of textual traces, often seemingly insignificant traces at that – fashion, gaslight, walking, mirrors, etc. In another, Benjamin's accumulations are like a Dickensian dust heap where we sift through the leftover bits and pieces of society, its ephemera. It is an unconventional reading of history in a project whose intellectual strategy is to dislodge us from conventional ways of understanding what constitutes history and, ultimately, what history is. Commenting recently on the *Arcades Project*, Simon Gunn says that Benjamin seeks 'to shake objects and events out of the continuity of history'.[42] What we are left with in the bundles of notes is a lack of cause and effect argument, and this is precisely the point for me: Benjamin's method of compilation and accumulation allows for new connections, unexpected moments of awakening in the present which come to us out of the traces and fragments of the past: what matters is how we assemble those traces. Susan Buck-Morss, who remains the most profound and profoundly original reader of the *Arcades Project*, suggests that it 'provides the reader with few answers as to Benjamin's intent but many clues, and these point ineluctably beyond the text'.[43] Another mystery of the city, you might say.

That is what I like about Benjamin – he allows us to go beyond the boundaries of his own text (however expansive those boundaries may be), to go (surreally) beyond the logic of cause and effect in order to embrace the tentative, with the possibility of sudden, unexpected connections. Let me put it another way. Benjamin grants me the freedom to pick from Benjamin, and here is what I choose: his emphasis on urban movement and walking and vision as a key (perhaps, still, *the* key?) to understanding the city, and his love of the fragment and the unseen connection; his method of putting quotation/citation alongside commentary and letting that link pose questions and suggest further unexpected meanings; his idea of the trace from the past which bridges the gap between past and present, and reconfigures history in so doing. Benjamin was in accord with many of the nineteenth-century writers he studied – Poe and Baudelaire, most obviously, but also Balzac, Dickens and others. The kinds of contingency and fleetingness and fragmentation that I believe define a variety of artistic expressions and representations of urban modernity are absorbed – accumulated you might say – in Benjamin's unending *grand projet*. It is here that Benjamin is at his least totalizing, where he allows boundaries to collapse, particularly those between past and present.[44] Perhaps this isn't so far from the vision we see in Baudelaire's 'The Swan', which, according to Benjamin, 'has the movement of a cradle rocking back and forth between modernity and antiquity'.[45] Benjamin's vision in the *Arcades Project* is one that not only allows for but also requires abrupt connections to be made. It doesn't have to provide a single overarching view of the urban world, but different routes within it. Benjamin's is an odd kind of philosophy, so odd that it might even be a queer one.

I am the ghost of Shadwell Stair.
Along the wharves by the water-house,
And through the dripping slaughter-house,
I am the shadow that walks there.

Yet I have flesh both firm and cool,
And eyes tumultuous as the gems
Of moons and lamps in the lapping Thames
When dusk sails wavering down the pool.

Shuddering the purple street-arc burns
Where I watch always; from the banks
Dolorously the shipping clanks,
And after me a strange tide turns.

I walk till the stars of London wane
And dawn creeps up the Shadwell Stair.
But when the crowing sirens blare
I with another ghost am lain.

Who is this ghost that haunts Shadwell Stair, that walks the
wharves with firm flesh? Why does he prowl through the night until
dawn? What is it he 'watches always'? Would we recognize this
man on the street if we saw him?
    What was Wilfred Owen thinking?

Chapter Two

Cruising Modernity

Queer Turns

Queer experiences have always been remembered, if remembered, as fragments and traces. In conventional cultural histories and in the stories of our cities variously told, queer encounters have remained footnotes at the bottom of the page, notes and queries in the margin or unarticulated suggestions lingering in the mind. That is, at best. At least as frequently, the traces of queer experiences have been lost in history – written out completely – and forgotten in cultural memory. Only relatively recently has the history of the invisible or marginalized been something we have named and considered worth documenting. The difficulty in writing queer history (as with any history, in fact) is in getting the story down without levelling it out. How can we tell a story without unnecessarily negating other, linked stories that might also be told? Where are our priorities? The grand narratives of modernity – and the use of the *flâneur* as a way of conceptualizing the experience of urban modernity – make such connections extremely difficult to establish. They prevent particular stories from being told. Specific and particular questions – questions like, what does it mean when two men look at each other in the streets of the modern city? – become more significant when the intention of writing history is to disrupt and to disturb the ways we have come to understand the events and people of the past. Disruption is the key to understanding the queer critical turn.

The emergence of queer politics in the late 1980s and early 1990s was one of the most forceful responses to AIDS in the West – a way of galvanizing anger and responding to the demonization of queer sexual practices that avoided divisive categories such as 'gay' and 'lesbian' and 'straight' and sought to bring together all kinds of people into a 'Queer Nation' of resistance, a broad coalition of disturbance which took many forms – new kinds of writing and thinking, particular forms of direct action politics, an in-yer-face visibility by the disenfranchised. And yet, what 'queer' actually means can still appear ambivalent, and purposefully, helpfully so.

Many recent works of cultural history focus exclusively on gay male history, lesbian history, or other histories, using the terms derived from identity politics as a conceptual political framework for understanding the world.[1] There are many reasons why gay history had, and still has, to be written; the need to document the stories of gay men and lesbians and other sexual dissidents remains. And there are many gay stories, but the story that touches my subject is the one about urban migration, the move of the marginalized from the country to the cities and capitals of America and Europe, many of which represented a New Gay Jerusalem (or Gay Mecca?) by the end of the twentieth century. San Francisco. New York. London. These cities had long established and thriving queer cultures and cultures of sexual dissidence, which have become the subject of academic and popular studies seeking to put gay urban history on the map. One of the most recent and celebrated of these is George Chauncey's *Gay New York*, an excellent account of the emergence of the shifting borders and boundaries of varied and overlapping gay (male) cultures in New York in the first half of the twentieth century. Other kinds of gay writing, in particular autobiographies and memoirs, have also helped to establish the experiences of gay lives in the city.

But imagining and writing a gay history is not the same thing as imagining and writing a queer history, although the two are often elided and they share some of the same goals, most obviously a broadly anti-homophobic politics. John Howard, author of *Men Like That*, a study of the queer American South, articulates this difference nicely:

> Queer is a useful rubric. Today it is often deployed ideal-istically, if sometimes problematically, to aggregate varied persons based on their myriad experiences of difference and outsider status – a coalition of the marginalized. I find that queer further opens up interpretive possibilities as we study the past. To speak of a gay history, to consult gay sources, and to query gay individuals often serve to perpetuate gayness as a category. To look for the queer, as variously conceived and embodied, in the past, might well result in richer and more accurate histories of deviancy and normalcy and might help denaturalize their present-day iterations.[2]

Queer approaches to understanding the past and present may avoid that levelling out of history I suggested above, may lead us to think outside the grand narratives that continue to see terms such as 'men' and 'women' in more or less uncomplicated ways. These approaches get us beyond binary thinking ('gay' and 'straight'), of the sort that has defined so much of the way urban modernity is understood. Furthermore, queer stories – stories that deviate from the norm, whether in content or approach – may help us understand the world we live in differently, even if (espe-cially if) that new world suddenly seems unfamiliar, uncertain and strange. Uncertainty can often be a good thing; so, too, estrange-ment. Specifically 'gay' stories still need to be told, for political and other reasons and in as much as all people need to have their stories told. But it is also worth reminding ourselves, as Howard does, that a gay history is one circumscribed by the category of gayness, and that gay narratives, no less than other kinds, have their own shapes – the coming-out, confessional narrative; the urban migration story; the liberation trajectory, to name a few. Queer approaches to writing and other cultural production seek less to define a specific and agreed upon historical narrative than to offer possible, contingent ways of reading the past in order to engage with the present in ways that do not rely on normative ideas and behaviours. Indeed, to 'queer' history is to challenge, undermine, refute and reconfigure the very notion of norms in 'history'.

One outcome of queer approaches to understanding culture and history is that we may be led to believe in the political potency of a *less*, rather than more, certain world, one that opens up a space for interpretation that considers the familiar and the unfamiliar in ways we don't always expect. Thought about in that way, it makes sense to me to bring together Walter Benjamin's dialectic and the political aims and radical uncertainties of queer theory. It is one reason I find Benjamin's ideas about the city of modernity so provocative and appealing – the Benjamin who embraces contingency, ambiguity, randomness and the unlooked-for in the *Arcades Project*. It is Benjamin more than anyone else who has considered the fragment and the trace as a basis for understanding of past and present. It is in that unfinished work that we can look for the queerly modern understanding of the city.[3] Benjamin's modernity is a contingent one. My own queer reading of the city is one in which the spaces of modernity are up for grabs and always liable to be contested and appropriated; in which the overlapping passing moments on the streets imply many ways of moving and seeing; in which the city allows for alternative and divergent kinds of experience. Cruising is a practice that exploits the ambivalence of the modern city, and in so doing, 'queers' the totalizing narratives of modernity, in particular, *flânerie*.

Neil Bartlett – novelist, translator, theatre director, performance artist, cruiser – has written what I take to be a model of queer cultural history and personal narrative, a work that captures precisely the vision of the queer city of modernity that I find in Benjamin's *Arcades Project*. Bartlett's *Who Was That Man? A Present for Mr Oscar Wilde* (1988) is part biography, part autobiography, part detective narrative. He writes from the position of a gay Londoner in the 1980s who wonders how he got there, how the behaviours and habits that define his world were established a century before, in the 1890s during the heady days of Oscar

Wilde. Bartlett's unconventional narrative can be read as yet another kind of gay narrative, an exploration of how one man's gay identity gets established, and also as a corrective of all the gay male stories that lean too heavily on the American Stonewall trajectory for their shape. Fair enough, then, to think of Bartlett's concerns as 'gay'. However, what is more interesting for me is his way of doing it, which makes the forgotten stories of the past crucial to the way we understand the present, by forcing a collision between the lost traces of history and the shape of contemporary experience. Take the dedication:

> This book is in loving memory of Jack Saul of Lisle Street, Private Flower, Fanny and Stella, La Princesse Salome and her sisters and lovers, Mr Gibbings, the eighteen-year-old-fisherman, the Euston Road queen, Clibborn and Allen, and, of course, all The Boys.

Even as the book opens, Bartlett introduces individuals left behind in history, not individuals he can ever have known, but individuals he 'knows' through cultural memory and his own dogged research: Jack Saul, a late nineteenth-century rent-boy, linked to both the Cleveland Street male brothel scandal in 1889 and Wilde's trials in 1895; Fanny and Stella, two cross-dressing 'men in petticoats' arrested at the Strand Theatre in 1870, whose trial was another great scandal (they were acquitted); Mr Gibbings who hosted drag balls at Haxel's Hotel, and who appeared at the trial of Fanny and Stella; and all the rest, The Boys, then and now. Bartlett dedicates his work to these footnotes of history occupying the margins of the streets of London, and he asks us to see them as central to a different kind of narrative, and in so doing to understand London in the 1890s, but also the 1980s, anew. This is as much a book about how we understand our cities as it is about how we recover alternative life experiences.

Bartlett prepares us for the unconventional narrative that follows with a few introductory pages in which, in the form of a dialogue (very Wildean, that), he explains his thinking:

I think you're right when you say I should tell my story from the very beginning, but I'm sorry, this can't be a simple confession, I mean it's not even my story at all. Coming to London (and that isn't something you do just by stepping off the train; it takes years, believe me, it's taken me years), coming to London meant moving into a life that already existed – I started to talk to other people for the first time, to go to places that already had a style, a history if you like. What I've done, I suppose, is to connect my life to other lives, even buildings and streets, that had an existence prior to mine. This is in itself remarkable, because for the longest time imaginable I experienced my gayness in complete isolation, just like any other gay child in a small town. And now, gradually, I've come to understand that I am connected with other men's lives, men living in London with me. Or with other, dead Londoners. That's the story.

His story, like all our stories, is the story of others – the connections we make to those we know, the fantasies we imagine about those we don't know. Like so many urban stories, it is also a kind of ghost story, whose figures from the past haunt the present. Here is how our understanding of ourselves gets shaped:

You know that your knowledge is quite arbitrary. Your knowledge of the city is shaped by the way ex-lovers introduce you to their friends, by the way you hear someone's story simply because he happened to be in the same place as you at the same time. And eventually you build up a network of places and people, perhaps you discover a particular group of people, or you look for, or accidentally find, one man who focuses your life. I moved from clue to clue, from name to name and from book to book. I started collecting pictures and anecdotes. I bought four big scrapbooks and filled them with whatever texts or images I could find from the London of a hundred years ago. I went back to the picture galleries and museums I used to haunt when I was sixteen. Gradually I began to learn the geography and language of 1895 or 1881, to redraw my map of the city, to recognize certain signs, certain words. I began to see this other London as the beginning of my own story – and up till then, like a lot of other men, I'd seen America and 1970 as the start of everything.[4]

Other queer histories may be as yet unwritten, but they are not unrecoverable. Scott Bravmann, in his exploration of queer methods of writing history, suggests that 'queer cultural studies of history propose a new approach to thinking about the relationship between the past and the present, they investigate queer fictions of the past as interventions into the material present'.[5] Bartlett's pursuit of queer experience in the fragmented textual traces of the past is just such an approach, and one that requires a willingness to embrace the tentative and the plausible, but also the disparate. His imaginative link with late nineteenth-century queer London culture helps him, and us, make sense of queer experiences today. In order to understand how our own lives are part of and impact upon the social collective, we must, in the words of sexual historian Jeffrey Weeks, tease out 'the hidden connections, making sense of what often seems incomprehensible, or merely idiosyncratic'.[6] Imagining history differently requires such unconventional interpretative methods. In this way, Bartlett may be closer to Benjamin in his *Arcades Project* than to postmodern approaches to the self and history led by identity politics. As Benjamin suggests, the 'trace' brings the past nearer to us and so makes more immediate the connections between the past and present, perhaps especially those connections we have hitherto neglected. What Bartlett does in his London story, past and present, is bring together illicit assignations, sexual transgression, masquerade and men passing on the streets; he locates himself on a hitherto little-known map of the city. Anyone of us might look for other clues and traces and map an altogether different 'London', and that map would suggest altogether different ways of locating yourself in the present.

Urban Traces

Here is an urban trace from 1881:

> The writer of these notes was walking through Leicester square
> one sunny afternoon last November, when my attention was
> particularly taken by an effeminate, but very good-looking

young fellow, who was walking in front of me, looking in shop-windows from time to time, and now and then looking 'round as if to attract my attention.

This is the first paragraph of *Sins of the Cities of the Plain* (1881), one of the few books of exclusively homosexual pornography from the late nineteenth century, and it depicts, if not quite a Baudelairean allegory, then at least a common enough street scene: two strangers looking at each other as they walk through the city:

> Dressed in tight-fitting clothes, which set off his Adonis-like figure to the best advantage, especially about what snobs call the fork of his trousers, where evidently he was favoured by nature by a very extraordinary development of the male appendages; he had small elegant feet, set off by pretty patent leather boots, a fresh looking beardless face, with almost feminine features, auburn hair, and sparkling blue eyes, which spoke as plainly as possible to my sense, and told me that the handsome youth must indeed be one of the 'Mary-Anns' of London, who I had heard were often to be seen sauntering in the neighbourhood of Regent Street, or the Haymarket, on fine afternoons or evenings.[7]

It is a passage that helps us to imagine, if not quite reconstruct, a cruising scene in late nineteenth-century London.[8] In the pages that follow, the transaction initiated by this urban encounter is completed. The rent-boy Jack Saul — the same Jack Saul in the dedication to Bartlett's book — picks up the narrator; they go back to the man's bachelor flat near Baker Street; all manner of 'gama-houching' (oral sex) takes place and the narrator offers to pay Jack to recount his life story, embedded in the book as 'Jack Saul's Recollections' and which forms the largest section of the text. *Sins* is an unusual text, because while we classify it as 'porn' and while you still have to read it at a special desk in the British Library, under the watchful eye of staff who are presumably monitoring your autoerotic impulses, it is many things other than conventional pornography. William Cohen calls it a 'peculiar mixture of programmatic pornographic narrative with apparently factual, and potentially exposing, information'.[9] Indeed, a narrative in parts, *Sins* is part autobiography, part guide to homosex in London, and it helpfully concludes with short essays covering such topics as 'Arses Preferred to Cunts', 'A Short Essay on Sodomy' and 'Tribadism'. Cohen's discussion of *Sins* links it to the culture of scandal in the period, and Morris Kaplan very helpfully shows how it is embedded in a culture of cruising and other cruising narratives. But I want to think about it slightly differently, to consider how a text like *Sins* sits alongside other more ambiguous and uncertain texts about men on the streets.

The cruising scene which opens *Sins of the Cities of the Plain* raises an interesting question: how do we know cruising when we see it, particularly in the late nineteenth century? I have said that this opening scene is obvious enough in its representation of cruising, and a number of signifiers help us to interpret the encounter. Firstly, there is the sexual geography of the West End – particularly linked to prostitution of all sorts in Regent Street and Haymarket[10] – that suggests an economy of sexual exchange, which locates the two men in a specific context of sexual ambiguity and fluidity. The streets of the West End are uncertain places with overlapping meanings linked to entertainment, commerce, leisure and domesticity, and Jack Saul lived just above Leicester Square in Lisle Street (still a fluid street today combining queer and other cultures). Saul knows how to exploit the uncertainties of the streets in the West End, and leisurely window shopping provides him with a reason for loitering, or 'sauntering'. As Bartlett notes in one of the footnotes to *Who Was That Man?*, 'shopping and cruising become interchangeable activities in the city' and 'cruising is like window shopping'.[11] And so it remains. In his journals, Derek Jarman writes:

There was nothing more exciting than a stranger stopping and looking back and the chase ending in front of a shop window, mirrored in the glass; the long journey to his place or yours; cocks throbbing and minds racing. Slipping him out of his jeans and sucking his cock, the ecstatic kiss, the discovered tattoo. Wild as a boy can be, sparkling eyes, laughter, the taste of him, the sudden mad rush to orgasm after hours on a tightrope of sensation.[12]

Certainly, the shop window comes in handy for Jack Saul in allowing him to occupy the streets ambivalently. The combination of an understanding of a specific place with an understanding of a specific urban practice allows for – in fact, enables – cruising to take place. And the sexual encounter here is made plain enough – it is a wholly unambiguous scene and the different parts of this narrative trace (the sauntering, the window shopping, the location) add up to a clear understanding of what is going on. You are hardly surprised when the scene transpires in the way it does. It's a work of pornography, after all, with its own narrative demands.

But what if the parts don't add up? Surely sometimes a saunterer is just a saunterer? Occasionally, a window shopper is just a window shopper? How do we read other, less overt narratives of the streets in which men encounter each other? Not all chance encounters lead to gamahouching in Baker Street, as we see in this urban trace from *The Times* in 1876:

At Guildhall yesterday, Mr Arthur Cunningham, who at first refused to give his age or address, but who afterwards said he carried on business in Gracechurch-street, surrendered to his bail before Alderman Figgins and Alderman Nottage, charged with indecent behaviour to a lad named Henry Donoghue, in the employ of Mr. Game, butcher, in Cannon-street. . . . It appeared that Donoghue was looking in at a shop window in Newgate-street, when the defendant came up and stood by his side. While in that position, the boy alleged, the defendant behaved towards him in an improper manner. He called the defendant a 'dirty old beast', and threatened to fetch the police. The defendant ran across the road, but was followed by the complainant, and pointed out to a constable. They went up to him, and the boy charged him with an indecent assault. . . . On the way to the station the defendant denounced the charge of the boy as 'horrible and false', and said that rather than have such a horrible thing against him he would give £100. He actually gave the policeman a sovereign, and promised him two more. That bribe, on the face of it, seemed to tell against the accused, and no doubt it was reprehensible; but one's experience showed that there were timid, sensitive men who, though perfectly innocent, would recoil with horror at even the mention of such a crime attaching to them, and would give or promise almost any sum rather than have such a fearful charge made against them.[13]

This case of alleged indecent behaviour, like many others in the nineteenth century, was dismissed and the defendant left the court, we're told, 'without any imputation or stain upon his character'. Similar accounts (and similarly vague accounts) of indecent behaviour in parks, churches and trains, between men and men, men and women, men and boys, were not uncommon. Among other things, this particular article points to the fundamental difficulties in interpreting the increasingly confused markers of identity in London, the world's largest metropolis.[14] Although the Aldermen rule in favour of the defendant – despite his attempt to bribe both the young lad and the police officer – the reader is left to interpret what really occurred in Newgate Street. Was the young man Donoghue just looking at a shop window, unlike Jack Saul, for whom the shop window is in fact a tool of his trade, and a way of inhabiting the streets that affords him the opportunity to cruise? Did the man proposition the young lad in an 'improper' manner, mistaking Donoghue for another type of street loiterer? (What *is* proper behaviour in the streets anyway?) Or, was the young lad, in fact, really just a young man with an eye for the main chance, someone who understood the streets and knew that to loiter in front of a shop window could be ambiguously and recklessly interpreted by another man? The problem for us, as it was for Aldermen Nottage and Figgins, is that we cannot know for certain. What remains is a textual trace of an urban encounter in 1876, but a trace that seemingly defeats our desire to define the streets, at least with any certainty. We are left here, again, with the question: how does one distinguish a man cruising the streets in search of another man from any other stroller moving through the streets of London? In fact, it is precisely because of this uncertainty in the streets with its many kinds of strollers that our cruisers are able to wander (or window shop). However we account for this trace, conventional accounts of the *flâneur* fail to unravel the mysteries of this man in the street, fail to explain exactly what occurred between Mr Arthur Cunningham and young Donoghue in Newgate Street in February 1876.

The literature of London in the mid to late nineteenth century is full of ambiguous street-walking men, particularly at night, whose uncertain identities merge with the indecipherability of the urban text they inhabit. Take, for example, Dickens's *Our Mutual Friend* (1864–5); here, London is more bewildering and incomprehensible even than the great obfuscating foggy metropolis of *Bleak House* (1852–3). The young lawyers Mortimer and Wrayburn, bachelors who set up a warm home together, forever take to the streets – partly to relieve the tedium and monotony of contemporary life, partly to take pleasure in urban wandering, but partly because that is simply what bourgeois men do. The teasing possibility in the early chapters, that these *flâneurs* might be interpretable as cruisers, and the ambiguity about the nature of their homosocial relationship get subsumed, or perhaps refracted, in the love plot with Lizzie.[15] Less ambiguous, although still indeterminate, is R. L. Stevenson's *Dr Jekyll and Mr Hyde* (1886), a hyper-male urban narrative, in which all the men inhabit the shadowy gaslit world of London. In Stevenson's fragmented narrative, the men are always out on the street, but no reasons are ever offered as to why. What exactly do the bachelor cousins Utterson and Enfield do on their habitual urban rambles, when they walk to the 'end of the world'? Why are we told, when Mr.

Hyde runs wildly and extraordinarily through the streets in the middle of the night, and collides with a young child, that it occurs 'naturally enough'?[16] The text never fully unveils the secrets of the night, and the mystery of these street-walking men remains a coded mystery of the city itself. The closer we get to understanding the nature of these men's movements in the city, the less is actually revealed. Or, as the novel itself puts it: 'the more it looks like Queer Street, the less I ask'.[17] One of the other great street wanderers of the late nineteenth century was Wilde's beautiful and damned Dorian Gray, whose urban rambles tease the reader into imagining exactly what Dorian gets up to in the city. In a conversation with his decadent mentor, Lord Henry, Dorian recounts how he stumbles upon the theatre where he first sees Sybil Vane:

> 'You filled me with a desire to know everything about life. For days after I met you, something seemed to throb in my veins. As I lounged in the Park, or strolled down Piccadilly, I used to look at every one who passed me, and wonder, with a mad curiosity, what sort of lives they led. Some of them fascinated me. Others filled me with terror. There was an exquisite poison in the air. I had a passion for sensations. . . . Well, one evening about seven o'clock, I determined to go out in search of some adventure. I felt that this grey, monstrous London of ours, with its myriads of people, its sordid sinners, and its splendid sins, as you once phrased it, must have something in store for me. I fancied a thousand things. The mere danger gave me a sense of delight. I remembered what you had said to me on that wonderful evening when we first dined together, about the search for beauty being the real secret of life. I don't know what I expected, but I went out and wandered eastward, soon losing my way in a labyrinth of grimy streets and black, grassless squares.'[18]

Is Dorian a *flâneur* or a cruiser? He certainly bears the marks of Poe's urban follower, he's also a Baudelairean decadent, and yet we're never absolutely certain what it is that Dorian gets up to on the streets that take him east, to the docks and to opium dens. We simply don't know.

Walking the streets is a way to signify transgression, as it is for Dorian above, but the precise nature of that transgression remains unnamed. All of the characters in these different texts emerge from shadows; they usually engage men visually on the streets; they even express desire and longing: but still a fundamental uncertainty and ambiguous understanding of their relationship to the urban environment remains. I don't think we need to spend much time trying to pin down these nineteenth-century street walkers in terms of twentieth-century sexualities. Whether Dorian really is homosexual is not the point. Whether Mortimer and Wrayburn share a bed, or simply breakfast, doesn't really matter. The reductive critical move is to define them when there really is no way of knowing. What I want to emphasize is the need to explore the meanings of their urban movement, rather than speculating about a specific sex act that is never offered, and to accept their contingency as agents walking the city.

From *Flâneur* to Cruiser

In their post-liberation, celebratory guide for gay men in the 1970s, *The Joy of Gay Sex*, Charles Silverstein and Edmund White discuss explicitly the practice of cruising and offer a helpful 'how-to':

> There's an art to cruising and it has a lot to do with timing and with the eyes. Take eyes first. You're walking down the street and you pass a man going in the opposite direction. Your eyes lock but you both keep on moving. After a few paces you glance back and see that the man has stopped and is facing a store window but looking in your direction. If he's not exactly the partner you're searching for you'll probably register the compliment his stare is paying you but leave it at that.
>
> But if he does catch your fancy you may go through the little charade of examining the shop window nearest you.

After a bit, the frequency and intensity of exchanged glances will increase and one of you will stroll over to the other. There are a few safe and stock opening lines banal to the point of absurdity . . . After these preliminaries you may extend your hand, introduce yourself, ask him his name and suggest you have a drink together.[19]

Silverstein and White here seek to define this queer practice of everyday life that sheds light on the textual traces of the past. They make apparent that, to borrow the words of film critic Bruce Brasell, 'cruising is a reading practice, a visual reading that is often accompanied by a verbal one'.[20] Urban modernity has most frequently been understood through vision – how we look at others, how others look at us, the dynamics of the gaze. Partly, this was due to new technologies that emerged in the nineteenth century that seemed to privilege vision over other sensory experiences – new media including the stereoscope, photography and then the cinema. Jonathan Crary suggests that the rupture in observation – the emergence of a new way of seeing – occurred from about the 1820s, as people had to adapt to the technological and institutional demands of modernity: 'Over the course of the nineteenth century, an observer increasingly had to function within disjunct and defamiliarized urban spaces, the perceptual and temporal dislocalities of railroad travel, telegraphy, industrial production, and flows of typographic and visual information.'[21] Benjamin's *flâneur* is one response to the new world of signs in urban modernity and he becomes, in Crary's words, 'a mobile consumer of a ceaseless succession of illusory commodity -like images'.[22]

Furthermore, an urban world defined increasingly by density of population – of people who remain essentially anonymous and who encounter others mostly as strangers – required new ways of understanding the fleeting moments of modernity. But it doesn't follow that the way we look at others necessarily suggests fundamental estrangement and alienation, from ourselves and others. Georg Simmel's important essay, 'The Metropolis and Mental

Life' (1903), is concerned with the psychological effects of urban living, what happens to the individual 'swallowed up in the social-technological mechanism' of the modern city. According to Simmel, 'the swift and continuous shift of external and internal stimuli' experienced in the city takes its toll. In short, we become blasé and overwhelmed, unable to take it all in, incapable of consuming equally all that the city and its money economy offers up to our senses.[23] The rush of images and signs that confronts us daily as we walk the streets in a seemingly endlessly shifting landscape has a price, and 'The Metropolis and Mental Life' emphasizes the difficulties an individual has in securing 'the independence and individuality of his existence against the sovereign powers of society, against the weight of the historical heritage and the external culture and technique of life'.[24] This is the modern condition for Simmel.

Yet, in his work on the sociology of the senses, Simmel offers what I take to be a kind of resistance to the overwhelming implications of that condition. He links the significance of seeing to the everyday experiences of individuals in urban modernity and suggests that there are ways of living amid the violent ruptures of external stimuli that allow one to connect with others and hold alienation temporarily at a distance. Looking at each other, which Simmel calls 'the most direct and the purest interaction that exists,' offers us some relief because it 'weaves people together' and creates unity in the face of urban fracturing:

And this connection is so strong and delicate that it can only be supported by the shortest line – the straight line between the eyes – and the smallest deviation from this line, the slightest sideways glance, destroys the uniqueness of this connection completely. Here, to be sure, no objective trace remains left behind, as is otherwise always the case, directly or indirectly, for all types of relationship between human beings; the interaction dies in the moment in which the immediacy of the function lapses. Yet the whole interaction between human beings, their empathy and antipathy, their intimacy and their coolness, would be changed incalculably if the look from one eye into another did not exist – which, compared with the simple seeing or observation of the other person, signifies a new and incomparable relationship between them.[25]

For Simmel, the mutual exchange of the passing glance – that contingent, fleeting, Baudelairean moment – can be a vital point of interaction, an expression of togetherness rather than of alienation, of connection rather than separation. I am not sure that the interaction necessarily 'dies' in the moment the glance is lost – it may live on in a different form as fantasy or phantasy, of the kind we see in Baudelaire's 'To A Woman Passing By'. It also may lead to another kind of encounter, a sexual encounter that may be the outcome of cruising. What is significant – and I think revealing – is that we need not get trapped in the assumption that the visual encounters of urban modernity are necessarily alienating, that the act of looking is always already inscribed by the script of the city that suggests that walking and looking at others constitutes *a single* way of experiencing the city.

The cruiser's intention is to find in the passing glances in the streets that person whose gaze returns and validates his own. In his recent study of homosexuality and modernity, Henning Bech suggests that the city is a sexually stimulating environment. It is the sexualization of the city of modernity that not only allows for but also necessitates ways of interacting that are based on desire:

What is it about the city that stimulates? Surely that altogether special blend of closeness and distance, crowd and flickering, surface and gaze, freedom and danger. Others are defenceless vis-à-vis your gaze and you yourself are on display to theirs; you come so close to them that you can actually touch them, yet ought not to: a distance that incites you to overstep yet still maintain it; surfaces intercept gazes and turn into signals, and the flickering vibrates; the crowd generates feelings of supply and possibilities; the anonymity and the absence of immediate social control amplifies the feeling, and the risk of nevertheless being monitored and uncovered increases the tension. You sense this omnipresent, diffuse sexualization of the city and confirm it by designing your surface accordingly and by taking up a position, perhaps also by engaging in cruising and brief encounters.[26]

Cruisers have their own signals, their own ways of responding to the inherent sexualization of the modern city, and there is something unique in the cruiser's urban gaze, relying as it does on a 'welter of signs':

The gaze is combined with a different mobility; you can track, you can stop and pretend to be looking at windows, you can sit down on a bench and get up again, you can end up out at Chiswick. What is called *cruising* is this combination of gazes and movements, which at gay bars takes place in an enclosure and finds its proper territory out in the city.[27]

It is important to emphasize, as Bech does, that cruising is a *process* of walking, gazing, and engaging another (or others), and it is not necessarily about sexual contact. Sex may be the point of cruising for some, but cruising and having sex are different interactions. Cruising has 'its own rewards: pleasure, excitement, affirmation', as Bech says.[28] Roland Barthes makes a similar point in *Incidents*, his published journals recording his everyday life in the café culture of Paris and his fondness for street hustlers:

I went out at around six-thirty, for no good reason; in the Rue de Rennes noticed a new hustler, hair in his eyes, a tiny earring; since the Rue Bernard-Palissy was completely deserted, we discussed terms; his name was François; but the hotel was full; I gave him some money, he promised to be at the rendez-vous an hour later, and of course never showed. I asked myself if I was really so mistaken (the received wisdom about giving money to a hustler *in advance!*), and concluded that since I really didn't want him all that much (nor even to make love), the result was the same: sex or no sex, at eight o'clock I would find myself back at the same point in my life; and since mere eye contact and an exchange of words eroticizes me, it was that pleasure I paid for.[29]

Mere eye contact and an exchange of words: for Barthes, cruising hustlers is a distinct kind of urban practice, an end in itself with its own pleasures.

Still, the *flâneur* and the cruiser are often confused, and it can be difficult to distinguish one from the other. In his recent and very personal account of the *flâneur* in Paris, Edmund White blurs the distinction between *flânerie* and cruising. 'To be gay and cruise', he suggests,

> is perhaps an extension of the *flâneur's* very essence, or at least its most successful application. With one crucial difference: the *flâneur's* promenades are meant to be useless, deprived of any goal beyond the pleasure of merely circulating. Of course a gay man's sorties may end up going unrewarded, but he doesn't set out with that aesthetic disinterestedness – unless sex itself is seen to be pure: artistic and pointless.[30]

I think he's got it wrong, actually. Firstly, you don't have to be gay to cruise (in the same way you don't have to be gay to like Liza Minnelli). But it does help to be queer. Plenty of straight-identified men cruise other men. Secondly, cruising (at least as I am discussing it) isn't only about the goal of sex (as Barthes and Bech attest). Reciprocal gazes may hold their own pleasures for some, and the dynamics of the gaze may be erotic and stimulating precisely because it does *not* end in sex. There are many levels of erotic investment and fantasy that exist in the idea of the possible, the potential, but the wholly unrealized encounter. (Is there anything so disappointing as sleeping with someone you've eroticized in your mind only to find out that they're boring in bed?) Furthermore, as White himself

One of several vignettes illustrating Louis Huart's *Physiologie du flâneur* (Paris, 1841).

indicates, the cruiser is not disinterested in the crowd in the way the *flâneur* so clearly is; although their ways of inhabiting the streets may look the same, there is a very different conceptualization of what the chance encounter means. The cruiser queers the *flâneur*.

That the *flâneur* may *look* like the cruiser is, however, part of the problem. Perhaps this was the difficulty Mr Arthur Cunningham faced in Newgate Street, that day in 1876? In fact, the visual iconography of the *flâneur* and the cruiser is strikingly similar. The illustration above depicts a *flâneur* from Louis Huart's *Physiologie du flâneur* from 1841, one of the books that both Baudelaire and Benjamin draw on for their understanding of this Parisian character.[31] As the *Physiologie* describes him, the *flâneur* is someone with the air of doing nothing, completely at ease, untroubled by the world around him. And he loves to look. This woodcut captures his way of experiencing the city – he smokes leisurely, leans on one leg with no intention of going anywhere, and stares around him almost shiftily. He strikes a very particular pose. It is a wild historical leap, but instructive, to compare the 1841 *flâneur* with the young man shown opposite. He leans, rests his hand on his hip, holds a cigarette in one hand and stares out at the viewer.

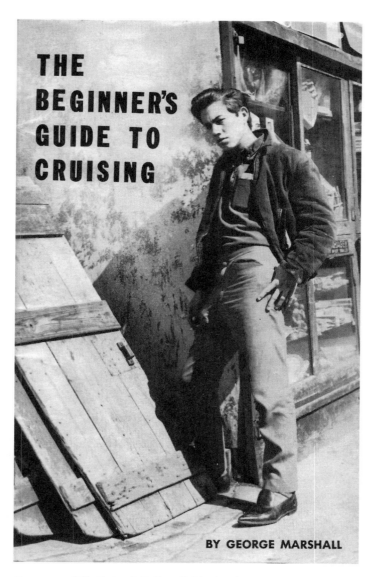

Front cover of *The Beginner's Guide to Cruising* (1964).

This photograph was published in 1964 (although it may have been taken earlier) and depicts a contemporary urban type, the James Dean type, the loner-male, stylish and confident, not bothered about the passing of time. The man we have just glimpsed is on the cover of a pamphlet published by the Guild Press in Washington, DC, publishers of gay pulp fiction in the 1960s and '70s. It doesn't attempt to be a very earnest guide, rather an account of cruising with tongue firmly in cheek. There are chapters on 'The Approach', 'The Moment of Truth' and 'How to Make Love'. The first paragraphs of the *Beginner's Guide* offer a brief sketch of what is called the 'tools and equipment' needed for the gay cruiser:

> What then must one have? Apart from the obvious gay attributes I would say that he needs time, freedom of action, a garconniere, some money, the gift of gab, imagination, self-control, a certain amount of cruelty, a bit of acting capacity, discretion, some taste – and that's about all. You might have noticed that I have left out some of the characteristics which are generally linked to the conventional idea of the cruiser: he need not be tall, handsome, young, impeccably dressed; not possess suave, courtly manners, extreme wealth, wit and intelligence. They all help, of course, but fortunately they are not as important as the more modest assets listed above.[32]

This isn't exactly the description of the nineteenth-century *flâneur*, and there are things that distinguish the two – the 'garconniere' (or bachelor's pad, akin to the flat in Baker Street in *Sins of the Cities of the Plain*) is superfluous to the *flâneur's* requirements, as is the gift of the gab. Look but don't talk, is his rule. Yet the cruiser and the *flâneur* are not that far apart – both with leisure time, a bit of money in their pockets, imagination, good taste and, especially, 'freedom of action'. Even in this wry account, it is not so much the physical attributes that matter – you can be old and short and ugly, which will come as good news to some – so much as the urban manner, the way of inhabiting the streets.

William Gedney, *New York, 1969*, photograph.

Look at two other examples of men on the streets. The one on the previous page is a photograph by the American William Gedney taken in New York in 1969. Who is this man in the photograph? Is he a hustler? Is he just hanging out on the street? Who or what is he looking at? We don't know, but we can guess that he wants to be noticed – he leans nonchalantly, suggesting availability, and the bare flesh sexualizes him, suggesting some intent in the pose. The image seen opposite is from a free pamphlet published in London by Camden Primary Care Trust, as part of a gay men's health campaign. It's the sort of pamphlet that you can pick up at gay bars and cafés, intended to fit conveniently in the hip pocket, and remind men of how to play safely when cruising and having sex (the two are inextricably linked in the guide). This is obviously a very different sort of guide from the *Beginner's Guide* of 1964, but the covers of both share the cruiser's pose with Gedney's man on the street.

In part, I'm being playful by putting the image of the nineteenth century *flâneur* alongside these twentieth- and twenty-first-century men, but there is a real question here, and one that haunts this book: how do we know our cruisers when we see them? I think the answer has to be that we don't, not always. While it may be true that cruising is more obviously interpretable and decipherable in the twenty-first century – because people like me write about it, because we see it in films and on television, because we read about it in the newspapers, because pop-stars get arrested, because there are cruising guides and websites – than it was, say, in the late nineteenth century, it is also true that our cities remain ambiguous places. The streets and other public spaces remain open to different kinds of users and to many kinds of overlapping social practices. The reciprocal, erotically charged gaze is still a significant way of making contact with others and of experiencing the city. The cruiser, like the *flâneur*, continues to rely on the ambiguities of urban modernity, on the uncertainties that linger in the fleeting experience of a backward glance.

CRUISING
FOR SEX

SEXUAL HEALTH FOR
GAY MEN WHO HAVE LOTS
OF SEXUAL PARTNERS

Front cover of *Cruising for Sex* (2003).

The first park in London I came to know was St James's, with its heavy, mature trees and unpretentious pond, and in the shadow of so many royal homes. This was in the summer of 1987. All parks have a past, in the way that all parks have a night-time, but mostly we know very little about either. Certainly, I knew nothing of St James's past, knew nothing of the prostitutes who used to frequent it in the nineteenth century, for example, knew nothing of its toilet where men used to meet. And it wasn't until many years later that I would come across this extract from Thomas Gilbert's poem from the eighteenth century, A View of the Town, in which a man leaves his wife on his wedding night to go cruising in the park:

> *Forlorn Saphira, with reclining head,*
> *Sighs for her absent lord in bridal bed;*
> *He to St James's Park with rapture flies,*
> *And roams in search of some vile ingle prize;*
> *Courts the foul pathic in the fair one's place,*
> *And with unnatural lust defiles his race.*

And so the poem goes on, linking Sodom and Gomorrah to London, worrying about the race of men prowling the streets and parks of the great metropolis at night. I've always liked the way the poem concludes, with its hellfire and damnation view of contemporary urban life:

Let Jesuits some subtler pains invent,
For hanging is too mild a punishment;
Let them lay groaning on the racking-wheel,
Or feel tortures of the burning steel,
Whips, poisons, daggers, inquisitions, flames:
This crime the most exalted vengeance claims;
Or else be banished to some desert place,
And perish in each other's foul embrace.

*I've often wished that Derek Jarman had made a short film
based on this little epistle – cut to an orgy of leather and spiky dog
collars. Cut to the legendary whipping tree on Hampstead Heath.
Cut to footage of an OutRage! demonstration. Jarman could have
done the poem justice, and turned it on its head at the same time.
One man's torturous punishment is another man's video.*

*In the same summer that I came to know St James's Park, I
lived in Earl's Court, but I don't recall anyone telling me about the
illicit, open-air pleasures nearest to me in Brompton Cemetery. It
was somewhere I only walked through on a few Sunday afternoons,
not a place I particularly connected with. I took photographs of the
roses and the choicer tombstones, like a tourist, and enjoyed that
special stillness that only cemeteries offer, but I never took much
notice of all the men walking through the paths (in jeans and
t-shirts and Doc Marten's). I simply didn't know. In the years since,
having moved permanently to London, I have come to know many
of London's parks and cemeteries in darkness and in light. Finsbury
Park, Waterloo Park, Highbury Fields, Abney Park – I have since
learned the secret histories of some of these places. But that was
all to come.*

*To begin with, it was a guidebook's London for me –
Westminster and the Houses of Parliament, Trafalgar Square,
Piccadilly, St James's Park – that first captured my imagination as a
young visitor. And perhaps a little oddly for a nineteen-year-old, the
street in my map of London that most intrigued and delighted me
was Jermyn Street, SW1. Here, running parallel to Piccadilly
between Regent Street and St James's Street is what I thought was*

the perfect London street, the quintessential London street. It is the kind of street you don't get all that often in London – several blocks long, but not too long (not long enough to change names, for example), and perfectly straight, to form a kind of catwalk, a runway – when you do get them, they're usually great streets. As a rule of thumb, in New York streets are usually much too long and much too wide, their monotony only broken (if broken) by the shift in architecture or the general hubbub of the crowd. In Paris, they're either too wide or too narrow. But Jermyn Street is an easy sort of street; it demands your leisure. Then as now, it is a street that largely looks after the needs of men – gentlemen – which is to say, very few men, broadly speaking. Snootiness combined with great attention to quality; clothes designed for eternity. The great shirtmakers like Turnbull & Asser, the old barber at Taylor's, Tricker's the shoemaker, a few murky looking restaurants, tobacconists. 'No Brylcreem down there; it's all very Gentleman's Pomade', says a character in one of Neil Bartlett's novels. Stripes everywhere – suits, ties, shirts, boxer shorts, dressing gowns – all intended to be worn at once in a riot of verticals. This sartorial mayhem was nicely in tension with the otherwise discreet nature of the street and its patrons. English rowdyism, but well fitted and smart.

There is now a statue of Beau Brummell on Jermyn Street, which attests to the street's whiff of decadence and a love of display. But it's only a whiff. Knightsbridge, it isn't. It's a quiet sort of street, a street that lies in waiting for discreet retail encounters. You can slip into Fortnum and Mason's by a back entrance off Jermyn Street, which is a telling gesture. This is the street I walked down many times when I first visited London, without ever, I think, actually entering the shops. It was enough for me then to watch those who did. I made do with window shopping.

On subsequent visits to London – a week or two here, a couple of days there – I always returned to Jermyn Street (almost never to Earl's Court), to pick up where I had left off. I don't know whether the shops we find in Jermyn Street today have actually been there forever, or whether they just look that way – is it true that Thomas Pink only opened in the 1980s? – and that's not really the point.

As I have imagined it, Jermyn Street epitomizes something about London, something intangible but alluring. There are many ways of explaining this allure – I wouldn't be the first American to be seduced by the presentation of old, fastidious London, to romanticize a past that wasn't mine and that is so much a fiction anyway, and one that was really about surfaces rather than depth. But the more I learned about Jermyn Street, the more interested I became, less for what appears on the surface than for what lies hidden in its past. No longer simply a place selling the perfect shirt and leather-smelling colognes, Jermyn Street increasingly became a place of mysteries . . .

Chapter Three

London: Mysteries of the Passers-by

Jermyn Street, SW1

More 'MYSTERIES.' – An incident of considerable gravity has recently occurred in London, which has hitherto been carefully kept concealed, but which in the interests not less of the victim than of the public, who have a right to look for a certain amount of security in the streets, should no longer be kept from publicity. Mr John Bateson . . . was walking through Jermyn Street about 10 o'clock on the evening of Friday, the 30th of June. Suddenly, and without his having had the slightest warning, some person came behind him and dealt him with some instrument a fearful blow, which felled him senseless to the ground. . . . The police, having been informed of the affair, have up to this time absolutely failed to obtain any information with regard to it; and this being so, it only remains to see whether the publication of this account may not lead to the discovery of the assailant guilty of this most cowardly outrage.[1]

This incident, along with one other which had occurred in Jermyn Street[2] two days previously, to none other than the victim's brother-in-law (by some unlikely urban coincidence) – became know as the 'Jermyn-Street Mysteries', for a brief moment in July 1876.

There is certainly something unusual about the mysteries – that two men are walking down Jermyn Street at night, alone, and get attacked is a misfortune; that they should be men of the same family looks like carelessness. We could ask, why them? Why this crime? Why then? But what interests me is, why there, why this street? Let me say now, that I don't know the answers to any of these questions with any certainty. As far as I know, this is all there is on record about these mysteries; it was a case that was never solved, just the sort of occurrence that you read about in the newspapers from day to day that lets you know that your city is a strange place. 'We are accustomed to think,' the article states, 'that life is pretty safe in this highly civilized age, and in the thoroughly policed town; but such cases as those to which we have referred are certainly well calculated to shake our belief in the accuracy of this conclusion.' As it happens, it is the unsolvability of the case that is compelling, the peculiarly ambiguous nature of the mystery of the passers-by in Jermyn Street that is so appealing. While we cannot solve this case, we can wonder what those men were doing on Jermyn Street, and why they were singled out. And we can hope to gather other traces and clues and perhaps even make sense of it in that way.

Here is another trace of Jermyn Street, from Anthony Trollope's short story, 'The Turkish Bath', published in *Saint Paul's Magazine* in 1869:

As everybody has not taken a Turkish Bath in Jermyn Street, we will give the shortest possible description of the position. We had entered of course in the usual way, leaving our hat and our boots and our 'valuables' among the numerous respectable assistants who throng the approaches; and as we had entered we had observed a stout, middle-aged gentleman on the other side of the street, clad in vestments somewhat the worse for wear, and to our eyes particularly noticeable by reason of the tattered condition of his gloves. A well-to-do man may have no gloves, or may simply carry in his hands those which appertain to him rather as a thing of custom than for any use for which he requires them. But a tattered glove, worn on the hand, is to our eyes the surest sign of a futile attempt at outer respectability. . . . In this instance the tattered glove was worn by a man; and though the usual indication of poor circumstances was conveyed, there was nevertheless something jaunty in the gentleman's step which preserved him from the desecration of pity. We barely saw him, but still were thinking of him as we passed into the building with the oriental letters on it, and took off our boots, and pulled out our watch and purse.[3]

Located in the neighbourhood of the gentlemen's clubs and shops catering for middle-class men like 'Jones from Friday Street' and 'Walker from the Treasury', the sensuously mysterious and ornately decorated baths were a place of male leisure and pleasure in the heart of the West End. In the action that follows the opening quoted above, a magazine editor is approached in the baths by a hopeful hack – in fact, the man he has seen across the street – who follows the editor into the bathhouse, hoping to place his literary wares in the editor's magazine.

Trollope's story was, in part, a gesture at topicality, capitalizing on the revived fad for Turkish Baths that occurred in cities and towns throughout Britain in the 1860s. The Hammam on Jermyn Street was just one of many other baths that were built in central London, and while this one was men-only (and remained so until it was demolished in the Blitz in 1941), others were for men and women, and baths targeted both the middle and lower classes. David Urquhart, a Scottish diplomat, was largely responsible for the Turkish Bath 'movement' at mid-century; he published pamphlets and gave lectures advocating the return to this ancient method of bathing and maintaining good health. Diseases linked to the skin, heart, liver, kidney, lung, stomach, virtually all the internal organs, in fact, were said to be aided by the baths. 'Diseases which peculiarly recommend to sufferers the use of the hot-air Bath' included syphilis, claimed one enthusiast, in addition to other ailments (related to feminine hygiene, for example) that it was not decent to discuss in the public forum of a pamphlet.[4] According to a newspaper report of a speech by Urquhart, one of the chief benefits of the ancient baths was that they allowed social classes to mix:

Speaking of the advantages of perfect cleanliness among all classes, the author pointed out that our intercourse with the lower orders was broken off by there being no settled occasions on which we are in contact with them, and by the want of cleanliness in their persons. In the bath both classes were constantly brought into the presence of each other. Contempt and distaste were removed on one side, degradation and irritation on the other.[5]

Elsewhere Urquhart, again discussing ancient practices, is quoted as saying:

The bath is essentially sociable, and this is the portion of it so appropriated; this is the time and place where a stranger makes acquaintance with a town or village. While so engaged, a boy kneels at your feet and chafes them, or behind your cushion, at times touching or tapping you on the neck, arm, or shoulder, in a manner that causes the perspiration to start.[6]

Urquhart wished to maintain that cross-class mix in the baths he constructed, a goal that he generally achieved. In Trollope's story, once inside the baths, the hack becomes uninterpretable to the editor because he is naked – without his 'tattered gloves' and the other markers of his shabby position, the editor has few clues and so doesn't recognize him at first. The baths have the potential to level out social determinants such as class.

What is striking in the opening paragraphs is the passing glance, and the way it forms the central dynamic of the action – it is the chance encounter that lingers in the mind, which propels the narrative – 'we barely saw him but still were thinking of him' – and which the editor is still thinking about while getting undressed. The first third of the story takes place in these baths, well known for what Trollope calls the 'picturesque orientalism' and 'very skilful boys who glide about the place and create envy by their familiarity with its mysteries'.[7] What takes place inside Trollope's homosocial baths, where skilful, young boys tend to their client's needs, is business and talk of business:

> 'How unintelligible is London! New York or Constantinople one can understand, – or even Paris. One knows what the world is doing in these cities, and when men desire.'
>
> 'What men desire is nearly the same in all cities', we remarked, – and not without truth, as we think.[8]

The 'truth' is that men desire money, in cities the world over. Another truth – although one that Trollope almost certainly didn't intend to explore – is that men are prepared to seduce other men, sometimes naked in a Turkish Bath, in order to get the money they so desire. As I have argued elsewhere about this story, the linking of money with desire suggests an undertext of sexual exchange: the editor is approached by a man who spots him in Jermyn Street and follows him into the baths, in order to 'sell' him something. Furthermore, the young, oriental boys, the heat, the steam, the nudity, the silence, the supply of men – all this is the stuff of cruising.[9]

There is only so far we can take the argument that beneath the surface of Trollope's bathhouse story is embedded a sexually latent tale – one which posits at least the possibility of the sort of steamy male encounters that are so significant to queer urban experiences in the twentieth century.[10] It remains tantalizingly ambiguous – the more the story heats up, the more it distances itself from the implications of the initial encounter, posited on the erotics of the street gaze. But this quizzical urban encounter in Jermyn Street and at the baths, the stolen glance of another man on the street that lingers in the mind, ought to be regarded with some consideration of place – an understanding of the urban location helps to fill in our gap. And knowing something about Jermyn Street at least provides a context for the men's encounter in the story.

From the time it was built in the early 1860s, the Hammam was a chief attraction of the street for its male visitors – not least because of the impressive and ornate Orientalism of the architecture – and it provided an important service for the clubmen of St James. Jermyn Street had always been a street known for pleasure and service. Developed during the Restoration by Henry Jermyn, the pleasure-loving Earl of St Albans, it provided shops and services for the residents of the grand townhouses nearby. Jermyn had just finished developing the land between St James's Park to the south and Piccadilly to the north, known as St James's Field, the showpiece of which was St James's Square, and which became one of the most prestigious addresses in central London, 'the first aristocratic development on such a scale in the West End'.[11] Jermyn Street's early residents included the Duchess of Richmond, a future Duke of Marlborough, various Earls, and other notables such as Isaac Newton, and it remained a fashionable address for the aristocracy and others for several centuries to come.[12] Commerce mingled with the formidable residences of the area, in both retail shops, hotels and in fairly well known brothels, all of which were there to serve not only the residents but also the gentlemen of the clubs. Eventually, arcades were built – the Piccadilly Arcade and the Prince's Arcade – connecting Piccadilly to Jermyn Street (these still exist, though they are not as fine as the much older Burlington Arcade on Piccadilly), offering more opportunity for luxury window shopping. When the Turkish Bath was built, it added to the services rendered by the street. In a guide to the area, Joan Glasheen suggests that Jermyn Street:

> . . . seemed an integral part of this man's world, where the English gentleman can still stroll to his shirtmaker or wine and cigar merchant, consider antiques and old masters, visit his tailor, hatter, barber or shoemaker – all within a short distance of his club. Truly a smooth, purring, exclusively male preserve, quite unlike anywhere else in the world. Henry VIII, and indeed, Charles II, would have greatly appreciated all that Jermyn Street offers.[13]

Trollope's story of the bath alludes to the kinds of encounters that take place inside, but it describes another kind of male encounter, too, perhaps another kind of male pleasure – the pleasure of the homosocial gaze on the street outside. It is worth seeing 'The Turkish Bath' and the 'Jermyn Street Mysteries' in *The Times* in relation to one another, and in relation to any number of other narrative traces which help fill out the picture of men on the street. What links Trollope's story and the 'Mysteries' is a street that men walk down leisurely, in a particularly male area of London, that caters for men's pleasures. And what we find when we accumulate the traces of Jermyn Street – when we locate those moments of reflection that appear in a shop window – is a particularly significant street in the queer map of the West End. A street that Jack Saul almost certainly would have sauntered down.

Jermyn Street and the area around St James has continually been reimagined and appropriated queerly. By the 1890s, the Hammam in Trollope's story was a well-known gathering place for Guardsmen and their admirers; when the Guardsmen arrived is difficult to determine, but it probably didn't take long for the semi-public space of the Baths to be converted to private use. In his photo history of queer life since the nineteenth century, which includes an 1862 image of the Hammam from the *Illustrated London News*, James Gardiner notes that 'uniformed Guardsmen notoriously supplemented their pay by working as prostitutes. *Queen* called this form of trade "a bit of scarlet"'.[14] The extent of the Guardsmen's presence is difficult to determine, since part of their attraction was in their bright uniform, which would have been lost in the nude environment of the baths.[15] They were perhaps more likely to be found loitering in Trafalgar Square, where a man in uniform was practically a byword for prostitute; certainly that was an established practice in the twentieth century. Still, Derek Jarman, writing in one of his memoirs, tells us that:

as a young MP, Harold Macmillan – who was expelled from Eton for an 'indiscretion' – used to spend nights at the Jermyn

Street baths; anyone who went to them would have been pro-positioned during the course of an evening. I went there myself on two or three occasions. They were a well-known hangout: dormitory and steam rooms full of guardsmen cruising.[16]

Because the London and Provincial was levelled in the Blitz, the baths Jarman frequented must have been the Savoy Turkish Baths, which opened in 1910 and lasted until the 1970s, adding further to the pleasures of men in Jermyn Street. The building that housed the baths still stands. As Jarman makes clear, the street had earned a reputation as a site of queer social and sexual exchanges, and though he doesn't mention it here, there was a well-known toilet for cottaging nearby.[17] There is a nicely coded example of the Street's queer connotation when, in 1932, Michael Hill pub-lished a play called *Queer People*, about two schoolboy lovers (one of whom, it transpires, has a lesbian cousin who 'comes out' in the play) who meet a decade later and try to renew their relationship. The play ends with one of the men committing suicide in a flat in Jermyn Street. When he revised it two years later, Hill added a preface that sought to explain that he wrote the play in order to bring to the stage a sympathetic portrayal of homosexuality:

> In an age when sexual inversion is the subject of fifth-rate Music-Hall jokes made by sixth-rate comedians, it is, perhaps, asking too much of the public to give the tragic matter the very serious attention it merits, and I can only hope that one day, some man or woman with a greater knowledge and a more able pen than my own, will succeed in impressing people with the obvious fact that men and women with warped and stunted souls, can no longer be regarded as material for sniggers from gallery audiences, and be exposed to the social ostracism which, unhappily enough, is at present their fate.[18]

Queer People was never a hit, though it was revised and repub-lished in 1934, with a new title presumably intended to make the sexual content less overt: *Tragedy in Jermyn Street*. A seemingly banal title, unless you knew how to decode it, unless you understood the queer meanings inherent in the urban signifier, 'Jermyn Street'.

In another of his books that effortlessly brings together the queer traces of the past, Neil Bartlett's novel *Mr Clive and Mr Page* (1996) uses cruising in Jermyn Street, from the 1920s to the 1950s, to link the two main characters – a humble department store bookkeeper, Mr Page, and a wealthy, upper-class young gentleman who lives in Mayfair, Mr Clive:

> It was almost two months before Christmas that it happened, early November I should say – that's if you don't count the first time I saw him. It was only on the second occasion that I actually spoke to him, you see – the time that I did, literally, bump into him. It was my usual time for Jermyn Street – I say usual, I suppose in fact at that time I was only just beginning to go; the West End was a whole new world for someone like me, and the London and Provincial Turkish was part of it that I'd only just discovered. Anyway it must have been a Saturday afternoon, because that has always been when I've gone, and I was on the pavement just outside the door of the baths. I was just putting my gloves on – it was cold – and I must admit that I wasn't looking where I was going. There was another man, somebody who I . . .
> Somebody who I thought I recognised, and I was watching walk up Jermyn Street towards the Haymarket; and when he reached the corner he looked back over his shoulder at me, and then, obviously I looked away, because I didn't want anyone thinking that I was staring at them, certainly not a stranger, because it wasn't as if it was anyone I knew, and then this other gentleman walked smack into me and nearly knocked me over. Which was Mr Clive B. Vivian, C.B.V., as it said in the stone up over the door of number eighteen. Although I didn't know that yet . . .'[19]

The Savoy Turkish Bath, 1955, Jermyn Street, London.

The two bump into each other coincidentally a week later on Jermyn Street, outside the baths, and their conversation hints at their sexual desires:

> I explained about the London and Provincial, which he said he didn't know about. Then he asked me if they were 'any good'. I was quite careful when he asked me that, and said well, yes, they were, and that you could get a massage, and so on.[20]

Bartlett's novel is particularly strong at recreating the cruising street walkers in London in the early and middle part of the twentieth century – the kind of man in the photograph from the 1950s shown in the illustration opposite. Who is he? What is he doing on Jermyn Street? Just window shopping? Does he go to the Savoy Baths? Does he know that Rock Hudson was thrown out of the Savoy Baths in 1952, for having sex with another man?[21] Perhaps this man was there that day? All of these seemingly banal questions take on a different meaning with some knowledge of Jermyn Street's history. *Mr Clive and Mr Page* very knowingly taps into the ambiguous sexual history of Jermyn Street that extends back to the 1860s when the baths were built. Like his earlier work, *Who Was That Man?*, *Mr Clive and Mr Page* is about cultural recovery and the mythologizing of urban cruising and the fleeting encounter.

More interesting still, Bartlett's novel suggests that shared, collective cultural memory is crucial for understanding the continuity of communities, not least queer people so often marginalized in mainstream accounts of urban life. *Mr Clive and Mr Page* opens with a long extract from a manuscript supposedly in the Victoria and Albert Museum, 'The Making of a House: The Story of Eighteen Brooke Street' by C. Beauchamp Vail, written in 1910:

> Men are ever seeking their comforts and to achieve their ideals. Ours is a home-making, home-loving race. I think that the desire is in all of us to receive the family home from the

A window shopper in Jermyn Street, 1955.

past generation and to hand it on to the next with some good work of our own visible upon it. Rarely can this be accomplished in times of rapid change. Families cannot hold and have not held even to the same localities much less homes generation after generation, but we can at least preserve some memory of the old. In times such as these the maintenance and due consideration of the hopes and works of the generations that came before us seems a duty all the more sacred.[22]

The history of Mr Clive's family home in Brooke Street is a history worth preserving because embedded in that history, as Bartlett imagines it, is also Mr Page's personal history. The 'sacred duty' which the chronicler of the house performs is analogous to that which Bartlett performs in writing the novel: both ensure that 'some memory of the old' remains for future generations. That the centre of interest is a bourgeois family home (in the United States, the novel was published as *The House on Brooke Street*, emphasizing its symbolic importance) makes Bartlett's queer appropriation of 18 Brooke Street all the more ironic and poignant. In a later extract from a book about the architect of the house, Bartlett quotes a commentator who described the new residence as 'a house with something to hide'. *Mr Clive and Mr Page* imagines the secret history of the house on Brooke Street, the memory of the house that weaves together an unlikely relationship between a lower-class clerk and a beautiful young aristocrat. Is the secret history true? Does that matter? 'Sometimes when I'm reading History,' Mr Page tells us, 'I stop and I wonder if I am being lied to.'[23] Throughout the novel – with its fictional recollections alongside fragments of what are presented as 'real' documents – the reader is often reminded that history (like memory) is only partial. As it happens, nearly all the extracts are *not* true, in the sense that Bartlett made them up. Of the Vail manuscript, for example, Bartlett says that 'like all the other documents in the novel (with the exception of the *Mirror* piece on the arrest of Rock Hudson), it's not a fact at all, but a fake. A fiction.'[24] These fictions may be true in other ways, however. Cultural history has a way of forgetting, and Bartlett's fiction acts as a reminder of that which might have been, and, at least in the queer imaginary, still is. Mr Page's story may not be history in the conventional sense, but it certainly preserves some memory of the old. Of steamy Saturday afternoons in the baths. Of stolen glances in Jermyn Street. Of the queer lives of previous generations.

We don't actually have to know the queer history of Jermyn Street and the baths to appreciate the novel, because we can still somehow believe that this specific street in St James, this specific place, with its shops catering for the pleasures of 'Jones from Friday Street' and 'Walker from the Treasury', is easily converted into private use. Jack Saul knew as much. Cruising on the streets of modernity turns on precisely the kinds of ambiguities explored by Bartlett and even by Trollope, who perhaps also understood the possible meanings of a backward glance on Jermyn Street. The site-specific queer-turn, combined with a reflection in a shop window, or a pause to light a cigarette, or sauntering at a leisurely pace – this is the moment when the cruiser seeks recognition in the eyes of another, what one writer at the *fin-de-siècle* would call 'the psychology of the moment.'

Ways of Seeing

A short story published in 1894 takes us round the corner from Jermyn Street to St James's Street, and develops the erotics of the cruiser's urban gaze more unambiguously than Trollope's story of 1869. 'A Responsibility' by Henry Harland appeared in the *Yellow Book*, edited by the expatriate American Harland and the art scene's *enfant terrible* Aubrey Beardsley (posing dandies, both). It positioned itself as the centre of the 'new art' and 'new literature', and emerged out of the culture of the experimental, provocative, very *modern* 1890s. It is in this context that the cruising in 'A Responsibility' should be read. As Beardsley and Harland tell us in advance of the first issue in April 1894, 'We feel that the time has come for an absolutely new era in the way of magazine literature. . . . Distinction, modernness – these, probably, so nearly as they can be picked out, are the two leading features of our plan.'[25] A new era, daring to be different and self-consciously embracing the modern is what the *Yellow Book* aspired to encapsulate and in some part define, and part of the way the magazine does this is through its exploration of the urban encounters and visual play in the streets of the city, particularly London. 'A Responsibility' is, when looked at in the context of the magazine, simply one of many different, overlapping kinds of encounters offered on the streets of the city. Harland's cruising narrative is embedded in all sorts of other stories of the streets, other ways of encountering others on the streets. What is so modern about the *Yellow Book* is the way it allows for multiple ways of looking and walking, some familiar, some less so, and the cruiser is shown to walk alongside many urban others.

The illustrations in particular established one of the dominant discourses in the periodical – having to do with vision and how to interpret what we see. Beardsley's images are the most playful, destabilizing notions of gender and sexuality in particular with their depiction of androgynes, imps, prostitutes and New Women. In fact, Beardsley frequently kept outré or downright porno- graphic images hidden in his drawings – an erect penis here, a vagina there – so much so that his publisher Richard Lane had to scrutinize them to make sure they were decent enough for pub- lication. Whether it is browsing, staring in the mirror, parading on the street, taking to the stage – the dynamic between spectator and spectacle (both in the content of the image and in the viewer/ image relationship) is always there. The dynamic of observing and being observed in the metropolis represented in Beardsley's images were significant to a number of other images in the *Yellow Book* that also emphasize urban spectating.

Walter Sickert's depictions of music halls, for example are precisely aligned with the periodical's wider interest in display, artifice, spectacle and urban pleasure. Sickert's painting of a Camden music hall, *Little Dot Hetherington at the Bedford Music Hall*, was published in the *Yellow Book* (volume 2) as 'The Bedford Music Hall'. In it we see how Sickert's visual play relies on unsettling the viewer through the use of mirror reflections which force us to question precisely what we are looking at and how we make sense of the visual encounter. In discussing *Little Dot*, Anna Gruetzner Robins points out that 'real and reflected images create spatial ambiguities' which work against absolute definition and precision; given that Sickert was in many ways a disciple of Whistler, this emphasis on urban ambiguity is no surprise.[26] As Sickert explained in 'The Language of Art' in 1910, 'pictures, like streets and persons, have to have names to dis- tinguish them. But their names are not definitions of them, or indeed, anything but the loosest kind of labels that make it poss- ible for us to handle them, that prevents us from mislaying them, or sending them to the wrong address.'[27] Sickert, then, is no less teasing in his way than Beardsley. He offers us scenes of urban entertainment and locates those places specifically, but also engages the viewer in a process of defamiliarization. While the nature of the ambiguities in Beardsley and Sickert are very different in their execution, both suggest the complexity of the relationship between stage and audience, between reader and text, in the city of modernity.

To some extent the *Yellow Book*'s focus on urban experience owes a debt to Charles Baudelaire, for whom the urban and the poetic were synonymous, and his shadow is cast in the periodical in significant ways. In a general way, the focus on urban visions in the *Yellow Book* – the theatricality and indeterminacy of Beardsley and Sickert, for example – can be seen in a line of urban cultural production back to the French dandy whose understanding of modernity was related to voyeuristic, see-and-be-seen urban practices at a time of material transformation. But Baudelaire's urban vision appears more obviously between the lines of the first volume of the *Yellow Book*, in Max Beerbohm's polemical manifesto for the 1890s, 'A Defence of Cosmetics', which echoes Baudelaire's 'In Praise of Make-Up', section 11 of 'The Painter of Modern Life.'[28] Baudelaire champions artifice over nature, and it is through women that the artificial finds its most potent expression:

> Woman is well within her rights, we may even say she carries out a kind of duty, in devoting herself to the task of fostering a magic and supernatural aura about her appearance; she must create a sense of surprise, she must fascinate; idol that she is, she must adorn herself, to be adored. It follows, she must borrow, from all the arts, the means of rising above nature, in order the better to conquer the hearts and impress the minds of men. It matters very little that the ruse and the artifice be known of all, if their success is certain, and the effect always irresistible.[29]

Despite what nineteenth-century realists might tell us, beauty, according to Baudelaire, comes from making-up rather than from imitating nature. Beerbohm's 'Defence of Cosmetics' makes similar claims, and artifice, perhaps even to a greater degree in Beerbohm, is what makes 'the modern' modern. Indeed, the rise of artifice sounds the death toll for the Victorian era:

> The Victorian era comes to its end and the day of sancta simplicitas is quite ended. The old signs are here and the portents to warn the seer of life that we are ripe for a new epoch of artifice. Are not men rattling the dice-box and ladies dipping their fingers in the rouge-pots?
>
> No longer is a lady of fashion blamed if, to escape the outrageous persecution of time, she fly for sanctuary to the toilet-table; and if a damosel, prying in her mirror, be sure that with brush and pigment she can trick herself into more charm, we are not angry.[30]

Men have become chancers (another motif in Baudelaire, in fact) and women have become artificial: such is the modern way. The prophetic voice of Baudelaire the dandy is rearticulated into a satirical, playful defence of the modern over a generation later, but through an emphasis on what we see, and how the object is presented for our visual consumption. It is all a performance, like the women making up in Beardsley's images, or the women on stage in Sickert's music halls. The world of urban modernity offers new sights for the sore eyes of the Victorian era.

That the city should be such a prevalent focus for the *Yellow Book* is not all that surprising, given the prominence of urban interests at the end of the century. In the early defining volumes, several contributors variously address ideas of vision and the city: as we have already seen, Beardsley and Sickert, but also John Davidson, George Egerton, Charlotte Mew, Henry Harland, Katharine de Mattos, Dauphin Meunier, Francis Forster and others. As the poet Richard Le Gallienne suggests, the 'interest in the town and urban things' was one of the defining characteristics of the 'general revolutionary Time Spirit' of the 1890s, and a 'cult of London and its varied life, from coster to courtesans' emerged.[31] Clearly, London was one of the great subjects for writers during the decade.[32] The *Yellow Book* did not initiate the interest in all things metropolitan, but many of the writers (including those listed above) associated with the cult of London certainly converged in the magazine's pages.

What emerges in the *Yellow Book's* range of urban depictions is a multiple city of modernity – there are different ways of being in the city and of representing it. But, the city as place of unexpected, random yet significant encounters is one of the dominant visions of nineteenth-century urban literature and it is captured in Charlotte Mew's story 'Passed' in volume 2. The narrator, who craves space, leaves her home and wanders the streets of London, as the dusk descends and the boundary between night and day blurs. Her exploration of the transformative period between night and day is reminiscent of Baudelaire (his poem 'Dusk', for example) and also of Whistler's mysterious *Nocturnes*. She happens upon a church where she encounters a young girl whose misery touches the narrator:

> My will cried: Forsake it! – but I found myself powerless to obey. Perhaps it would have conquered had not the girl swiftly raised herself in quest of me. I stood still. Her eyes met mine. A wildly tossed spirit looked from those ill-lighted windows, beckoning me on. Mine pressed towards it, but whether my limbs actually moved I do not know, for the imperious summons robbed me of any consciousness save that of necessity to comply.
>
> Did she reach me, or was our advance mutual? It cannot be told. I suppose we neither know. But we met, and her hand, grasping mine, imperatively dragged me into the cold and noisy street.[33]

This chance encounter – 'the magnetism of our meeting', as the narrator later calls it – leads her to a squalid room where the young girl's dead siblings rest. This confrontation with immortality that literally stares at the narrator – 'those dark eyes unwillingly open reached mine in an insistent stare' – sends her into a phantom reverie, and eventually she flees:

> My sole impulse was flight; and the way, unmarked in the earlier evening, was unknown. It took me some minutes to find a cab; but the incongruous vehicle, rudely dispersing the haggling traders in the roadway, came at last, and carried me from the distorted crowd of faces and the claims of pity to peace.[34]

Disoriented and lost in an urban land of the unknown (poverty, death), the woman returns home, where her brothers are laughing with friends and a waltz is taking place in the rooms upstairs. In the concluding scene, four months after the encounter in the church, the narrator finds herself among the throng of the crowd at a department store sale:

> The place presented to my unfamiliar eyes a remarkable sight. Brilliantly lit windows, exhibiting dazzling wares, threw into prominence the human mart.
> This was thronged. I pressed into the crowd. Its steady and opposite progress neither repelled nor sanctioned my admittance. However, I had determined on a purchase, and was not to be baulked by the unforeseen. I made it, and stood for a moment at the shop-door preparing to break again through the rapidly thickening throng.[35]

The 'human mart' and the thickness of the crowd suggests 'Virtue's very splendid Dance of Death', and as a 'sickening confusion of odours' assails her senses, she recalls the night four months previously when she confronted death and fled. In the city, one never knows when a chance encounter will take on deeper significance, as it does to an almost religious degree in Mew's story.

In volume 3, Henry Harland's story 'When I am King' similarly imagines the outcome of a chance urban encounter. The narrator here explores the labyrinthine city of unknown streets –

'I had wandered into a tangle of slummy streets, and began to think it time to inquire my way back to the hotel'[36] – when he turns a corner and is forced to confront his past. As in Mew's story, a kind of magnetism draws the speaker forward, and the sound of a piano playing lures him into a dive bar where he sits enraptured, undistracted by female attentions:

> I don't know why, but from the first he drew my attention; and I left my handmaid to count her charms neglected, while I sat and watched him, speculating about him in a melancholy way, with a sort of vicarious shame.

The sound of the music is the catalyst for memory:

> The tune he was playing now, simple and dreamy like a lullaby, and strangely at variance with the surroundings, whisked me off in a twinkling, far from the actual – ten, fifteen years backwards – to my student life in Paris, and set me to thinking, as I had not thought for many a long day, of my hero, friend and comrade, Edmund Pair . . . [37]

Pair is an old friend of the speaker's, indeed, the object of hero-worship for him, but a figure now tragic and fallen. He tells his story – of his marriage to a lower-class wife who dies (formerly she had been abused by her tailor husband) – but refuses to maintain his friendship with the speaker, preferring to remain detached and apart from such sympathy as figures from the past can offer. In Mew and Harland, chance encounters in the city are revelatory, exposing both the layers of harshness of urban life and the difficulties we have once the urban margins have been revealed. John Davidson's poem, 'Thirty Bob a Week', in volume 2, similarly points out that the city is a place of struggle for a worker whose life is viewed as a cycle of drudgery:

> For like a mole I journey in the dark,
> A-travelling along the underground

From my Pillar'd Halls and broad suburbean [sic] Park
To come the daily dull official round;
And home again at night with my pipe all alight
A-scheming how to count ten bob a pound . . .[38]

Reading through the early, defining volumes of the *Yellow Book*, what we notice is the range of approaches to depicting the city, an almost kaleidoscopic attempt to show the modern metropolis in all its multi-faceted complexity. There is a celebratory, exultant tone in George Egerton's story 'A Lost Masterpiece: A City Mood, Aug. '93' (volume I), in which a woman returns from the country to the city, eager to bathe in the multitude of the crowd: 'The desire to mix with the crowd, to lay my ear once more to the heart of the world and listen to its life-throbs, had grown too strong for me; and so I had come back . . .'[39] It doesn't get much more Baudelairean than that (except that it's a woman plunging into the multitude). Her engagement with the city takes the form of the common pose of the detached on-looker for whom the rush of undeciphered images, sights and sounds lead to reverie:

> The coarser touches of street-life, the oddities of accent, the idiosyncracies of that most eccentric of city-dwellers, the Londoner, did not jar as at other times – rather added a zest to enjoyment; impressions crowded in too quickly to admit of analysis, I was simply an interested spectator of a varied panorama.

For the narrator, the congested, chaotic imagery of the city is the raw material of poetic vision:

> The tall chimneys ceased to be giraffic throats belching soot and smoke over the blackening city. They were obelisks rearing granite heads heavenwards! Joints in the bricks, weather-stains? You are mistaken; they were hieroglyphics, setting down for posterity a tragic epic of man the conqueror, and fire his

slave; and how they strangled beauty in the grip of gain. A theme for a Whitman![40]

Whitman, of course, was one of the greatest writers of the city in the nineteenth century, a poet for whom the streets of Manhattan offered multitudinous opportunities to encounter the teeming mass of humanity. In Whitman's urban vision, reciprocal encounters with others are more significant than detached onlooking, and in Whitman there is a desire to connect with the objects of the urban gaze. For the narrator in Egerton's story, to engage with the contradictions of the external world of the city streets is, as in Whitman, to engage with the internal world of the self; the seemingly insignificant gets transformed into the deeply meaningful through the imaginative power of the self to (self-)create.

Harland's 'A Responsibility' offers us yet another way, the cruiser's way, of imagining street encounters in the modern city. It is a simple story – two men meet on holiday in Biarritz; there's an attraction of some sort which never gets explored other than through the gaze; they meet again on the street in London, where they remain separated despite their attraction; one of the men, Richard Maistre, commits suicide. The reader knows of Richard's death from the beginning, so the story is set up as the narrator's recollection of their encounters, in an attempt to determine the level of responsibility he must take for the suicide. In this way, it is a very Jamesian story, in which what does not happen has larger moral ramifications than what might have happened.

Like so many other urban stories, 'A Responsibility' relies on a dynamic of vision, whether on the city street or not. The narrator and Richard exchange glances and stares over the dinner table in Biarritz, always catching each other's eye. The narrator says that Richard was

the only member on whom the eye was tempted to linger. The others were obvious – simple questions, soluble 'in the head.' But he called for slate and pencil, offered materials for doubt and speculation, though it would not have been easy to tell wherein they lay. What displayed itself to a cursory inspection was quite unremarkable: simply a decent-looking young Englishman, of medium stature, with square-cut plain features, reddish-brown hair, grey eyes, and clothes and manners of the usual pattern. Yet, showing through this ordinary surface, there was something cryptic. For me, at any rate, it required a constant effort not to stare at him. I felt it from the beginning, and I felt it till the end: a teasing curiosity, a sort of magnetism that drew my eyes in his direction.[41]

In many ways, this is a definitive *flâneur*'s point of view, adopting the external world around him as a place to be deciphered – as a mystery in need of interpretation as in Poe's 'Man of the Crowd'. The narrator objectifies Richard, finds him curious, interesting to watch, appealing; yet, he tries (not very successfully) to remain as distanced as possible: 'I tried to appear unconscious of him as a detached personality, to treat him as merely a part of the group as a whole. Then I improved such occasions as presented themselves to steal glances at him, to study him *à la dérobée* – groping after the quality, whatever it was, that made him a puzzle – seeking to formulate, to classify him.'[42]

The point here, however, is that the narrator is simply unable to remain detached and aloof from his object because Richard continues to return the gaze, making stolen glances *à la dérobée* futile:

As I looked up, our eyes met, and for the fraction of a second fixed each other. It was barely the fraction of a second, but it was time enough for the transmission of a message. I know as certainly as if he had said so that he wanted to speak, to break the ice, to scrape an acquaintance; I knew that he had approached me and was loitering in my neighbourhood for that specific purpose. I *don't* know, I have studied the psychology of the moment in vain to understand, why I felt a perverse impulse to put him off. I was interested in him, I was curious about him; and there he stood, testifying that the interest was reciprocal, ready to make the advances, only waiting for a glance or a motion of encouragement; and I deliberately secluded myself behind my coffee-cup and my cigarette smoke. I suppose it was the working of some obscure mannish vanity – of what in a woman would have defined itself as coyness and coquetry.[43]

The narrator's anxiety here is created through an act of reciprocal vision. It is one thing to stare at someone to whom you are attracted, but it is quite another thing to have that person stare back, especially when their eyes seem to suggest longing. This is similar to other urban encounters in the *Yellow Book*. When the narrator in Charlotte Mew's story 'Passed' comes face to face with the pitiful young girl in the church, she asks: 'Did she reach me, or was our advance mutual?'[44] The urban encounter with the other is a fraught exchange, precisely because it *breaks* the rules of the city, forcing connection, rather than reinforcing separation. In 'A Responsibility', the message transmitted between the two men is untranslatable; the content of the stare remains undeciphered and so unspoken, and the visual never becomes the verbal. There is a clear spatial metaphor indicated – Richard *loiters* – a word resonant of casual sexual encounters – in the neighbourhood for a specific reason the narrator fails to understand. Finally, he understands his anxiety, comparing it to that of a flirtatious woman, making the sexual tension of the passage explicit through an act of imaginative gender reversal. Later, the narrator tells us that:

> I was among those whom he had marked as men he would like to fraternize with. As often as our paths crossed, his eyes told me that he longed to stop and speak, and continue the promenade abreast. I was under the control of a demon of mischief; I took a malicious pleasure in eluding and baffling him – in passing on with a nod. It had become a kind of game; I was curious to see whether he would ever develop sufficient hardihood to take the bull by the horns.[45]

The phallic imagery of the bull's horns is obvious enough; what is more revealing is that the narrator understands Richard's isolation and alienation from others, but views it all as a game. He knows that he can redeem Richard, can offer hope through mutual recognition by making the visual expressions of desire verbal, but he finally refuses.

The story ends with both men back in London, where they pass each other in St James's in the West End, in the centre of middle-class male pleasure, around the corner from Jermyn Street, where Trollope's men stare at each other before going into the baths. On St James's Street, the two men stop and stare, as is their wont, but the narrator chooses once again not to act or acknowledge the unspoken desires between the two men. The suicide note that Richard leaves is a simple one: "'I have no friends . . . Nobody will care. People don't like me; people avoid me. I have wondered why; I have tried to watch myself, and discover; I have tried to be decent. I suppose it must be that I emit a repellent fluid; I suppose I am a "bad sort".'[46] 'A Responsibility' is a cruising narrative, in which the 'cruise' is unsuccessful because the narrator refuses to acknowledge the full implications of the reciprocal gaze. In this way, he does not live up to his social responsibility – to connect with others, especially those who need it most. The psychology of the moment – the moment of desire – in urban modernity that so puzzles the narrator is a common one, but it is less about alienation than thwarted connection, less about detachment than a longing to be with another.

He fails to make verbal what seems so plain visually. The story is deeply revealing about 'the psychology of the moment', when two men's eyes meet and express illicit desire in St James's Street.

A few summers ago, when I was doing research for this book in New York, I sometimes went to a bar called The Cock in the East Village. It's like lots of bars in New York and elsewhere, narrow, cramped, loud, sweaty and (before the new laws) smoky. The Cock has something like a back room, but not like a raucous 1970s back room, or like some back rooms I know about in London, at least not when I've been there. The back room at The Cock is actually located in the back — not all are, some back rooms are in cellars, some upstairs, and some bars are so cruisy throughout they make you wonder what constitutes the front room.

One evening, when the lights were no longer dimmed and everyone was heading to the door and I was leaving (alone, as I had arrived . . . start as you mean to go on, except that's not at all what I meant), I noticed a digital sign by the bar suggesting that more fun might be found outdoors at Stuyvesant Square. I had never walked by Stuyvesant Square before, so it was particularly helpful that the notice gave its location. Stuyvesant Square isn't so much one square as two small ones on either side, east and west, of wide Second Avenue. But both sides were active cruising grounds, which is pretty impressive since there isn't much foliage, not many places to be discreet, and there always seem to be locals walking their dogs at all times of the night. The Cock pointed me in the direction of Stuyvesant Square and in that direction I went, partly out of carnal need, but also out of curiosity because by by a strange coincidence, in the New York Public Library at 42nd Street a few days before, I had been reading about Stuyvesant Square in the 1890s, where a young cruiser named Earl Lind hung out and flirted with adolescents who spent their evenings on its park benches doing whatever it was that fin-de-siècle American teenagers did in parks at night back then. The Cock was right, it was a good place to go at 4 am, and I went back again. It was often busy that summer – couples leaning by a tree here and there, occasionally a larger group in a circle jerk, but it wasn't what you'd call heaving. That was a few years ago, and I don't think it's like that any longer. Last time I was in New York, I walked down Second Avenue late one night and the gates to the little squares on either side were closed. I don't know where the neighbours walk their dogs now at night, but it isn't in Stuyvesant Square.

Chapter Four

New York: City of Orgies, Walks and Joys

Myrtle Avenue, Brooklyn

Although he hasn't disappeared without a trace, the photographer William Gedney is much less well known than he should be. If regarded at all, it is probably for his series of photographs of Kentucky, with its tender study of rural, southern masculinity, but he also produced important series of India, San Francisco and New York in the 1960s and '70s.[1] When Gedney died of an AIDS-related illness in 1989, he left a large archive of contact sheets, notebooks, sketchbooks and other materials now housed at Duke University in North Carolina. Anyone with an interest can take a look at the archive, but probably not many people do. Gedney is not exactly forgotten – because he was never in a particularly strong position to be remembered. He's a figure somewhat on the edge of the map of post-war American photography, eclipsed by others who were less self-effacing, more ambitious and self-serving, or just luckier. If we allowed it, it would be easy enough for Gedney to remain at the margins, as a footnote in the story of late twentieth-century American photography. But in the story that interests me and in the connections I wish to make, he has a significant role to play in my narrative of New York.

Let's begin with a trace from Gedney's notebooks, here described by their editor, Margaret Sartor:

> According to habit, he used a black fountain pen and drew two rules before and after, to define the beginning and end of

the entry. The cloth-covered hand-sewn book is titled 'Transcriptions and Notes.2' and is the second of a pair of notebooks, similarly formatted, that Gedney began in 1971. These were an ongoing documentation of what amused, interested, or provoked Bill Gedney: events witnessed, overheard conversations, dialogue from movies, passages from novels and newspapers (always attributed), his own curious mind. When he chose his own words, he would edit even as he composed, scratching out and rewriting a sentence until the description was not only accurate but pleasingly put. There are fleeting observations and long-winded monologues, unilateral arguments and self-admonishments. His handwriting suggests the flow of thought – for the most part intelligible, but sometimes hasty, unmindful of linearity, or wobbly and fading into scribbles. To record the personal fact, Gedney departed from black ink and used red . . .[2]

According to Sartor, reading the notebooks, one becomes 'mindful of juxtaposition and resonance, aware of the underlying narrative' and she believes that 'the entries are like snapshots: glimpses of thought, philosophy, insight, irony, fact, and humour that add up to a kind of scrapbook of Gedney's thinking'.[3] I like the description of the notebooks as glimpses, with a photographer's emphasis on how we see what we see. Indeed, many of his photos, whether of the city or not, often seem to be mere glimpses, although glimpses are never just 'mere'. He gives us glimpses of young men fixing a car in the middle of nowhere (which is, of course, somewhere) in Kentucky. Glimpses of hippies hanging out commune-style in San Francisco in the 1960s. Glimpses of the energy and vitality found on a street in Bombay. Glimpses of empty street corners at night. His notebook entries offer analogous glimpses, or traces of citation and commentary, juxtaposition, echo and reverberation. They are his own private *Arcades Project* and they present us with a montage of a life – of a gay man for whom the textual traces in a notebook were partly a way of engaging with and understanding his city, its past and present. The queer reading of his life exists in the contents of the entries, but also in the interpretative space between the lines.

Here is a long passage from one of the two notebooks Gedney kept while he lived in Myrtle Avenue, Brooklyn, recently published for the first time:

1969 Brooklyn Aug 20 Wed
Notes on the Street 'Homage to Myrtle Avenue'
Horizontal movement, the flow of commerce, path of goods and people.
Atmosphere: the change of light from left to right (east to west), reflected light, the pattern of light, rain, snow-storm — Turner.
Full-length figure: all people appear at a distance, the face becomes unimportant, the overall gesture of the figure; silhouette, the figure always appears in relation to the background or frame of the composition — Japanese prints — Brueghel (snow scenes, large scenes; scale the same).
Chance relationships: the inter-relation of strangers, beings unaware of their relationship to one another (example: the people on the elevated unaware of the man standing on the curb of the street, yet both appear within the frame of the camera, both exists in the same space and time).
Time: the passage of time, the endlessness of time, the patter of repetition, of daily actions, the patterns of traffic; (going to work, shopping, deliveries, children play in the street, coming home from work, the closing stores, etc.). the feeling of the day as a unit of time — awareness of time.
Distance: the objectivity of distance — the ant hill — masses viewed from afar, from above.
The use and purpose of streets: history.
Architecture of the street: a reflection of the people who use it.
The streets as a place of danger: a place of crime, of confusion, movement, speed, noise, many fleeting images confront the walker of the streets. A place where anything can happen.
The freedom of the streets: a place of democracy, of escape

from interiors, the mingling of classes, of high and low, the leveling ground of society.

Continuity of streets in a city, the endless feeling of one street leading to another, an ancient chain of physical communication.

Etiquette of streets: its manners, the watching of streets: the old, chance meetings, the insecurity of being in an open place, of vulnerability.

The death of the street: the dehumanization of the city street, unclean, crowded, unpleasant, the collapse of neighborhoods, place of strangers, unfriendly faces.[4]

It is easy enough to find in passages such as this a latter-day *flâneur's* understanding of the city and the streets. Like the street watcher in Baudelaire, the urban experience here isn't simply about the contemporary; rather, the streets suggest history, time and memory. Like Baudelaire's hero of modern life, Gedney transforms the fleeting into the transitory and makes the momentary permanent. Distance, watching, endlessness, movement, time – all of these are, in a sense, keywords for understanding *flânerie*. Perhaps the photographer as *flâneur* comes as no surprise since the role of the camera often appears (or hopes to appear) as a kind of passive onlooker, recording the environment rather than participating actively in creating it, particularly in strictly realist photographs that seek to capture the everyday life of the city. Gedney's photos are in part stolen images. He is a criminal in the way Poe's 'man of the crowd' is; he blends in. His pictures are so natural a part of the environment they seek to record that it is easy to forget the intervention of the technology and the photographer. Unlike the New York photos of, say, William Klein, whose vision has something in common with the ideas of the urban modernist Fernand Léger and who seeks to capture rhythm,[5] Gedney's city images are often quiet, still (not to say static), less crowded, often contemplative. The photographer seeks to hide and often disappears.

For Gedney, as for so many other urban artists, the street is the focus from which to imagine the complexities of the city more generally. It anchors the mind, locates and places it in a way that other abstract mappings of the city do not. The street is the base unit of the city. Gedney focuses on Myrtle Avenue in his notebooks, where he lives, and from which he imagines and records other places and people, other ways of thinking about the city generally. The Myrtle Avenue notebooks contain references to many other streets, often through quotations from a wide range of classic urban literature – including Flaubert, Henry Miller, Celine and Christopher Isherwood – and from city journalism, passages from *The New York Times* and *The New Yorker*, for example. Gedney is promiscuous in his use of citation, but the notebooks also appear as random (in the way promiscuity so often does). Just as meandering the passages in the *Arcades Project* is part of the point in Benjamin, so, too, there are a number of directions we might take in thinking about the Myrtle Avenue notebooks, but I will follow just one of the routes on offer.

On 8 September 1969 there is an extract from *The Brooklyn Daily Eagle* from 1888 about the popularity of chewing gum for commuters travelling from Brooklyn to Manhattan. It is interesting enough because it quite rightly links chewing gum to the rhythm of the city – it's rather like humming, something that is particularly suited to walking the streets. But that's beside the point, really; what first captured my eye about this article is its link to Walt Whitman. Gedney knew that from 1846 to 1848 Walt Whitman was editor of the *Brooklyn Daily Eagle*, and among Whitman's early articles and leaders for the paper are numerous short pieces on Brooklyn, the changing streets, the transformations taking place and the occurrences of everyday life, the sort of journalism represented by the brief article on chewing gum in 1888 that Gedney cites as significant. When Whitman was writing for the *Eagle* (and other papers at different times), Brooklyn was not yet a part of greater New York, not yet incorporated as one of five boroughs. It was its own vibrant city, with a population of around 200,000 by the 1860s, a city that one travel guide suggested was poised to become another London. Whitman loved his city and his job, and well before the first edition of *Leaves of Grass* was published in 1855, he was a jobbing journalist with a prodigious output. What appealed to him about the press was the idea of writing for the masses, or at least the many. Journalism was a tremendously democratic mode of expression for Whitman (as for many others), so it is no surprise that in much of his journalism, we see the eloquent poet-to-be, and in much of *Leaves of Grass*, we see the carefully observant journalist. As Whitman tells us in an article from the beginning of his tenure on the *Eagle*,

> There is a curious kind of sympathy (haven't you ever thought of it before?) that arises in the mind of a newspaper conductor with the public he serves. He gets to *love* them. Daily communion creates a sort of brotherhood and sisterhood between the two parties. As for us, we like this.[6]

I think we ought to take him at his word – in his way he *loved* being able to reach the unknown and unseen masses through the press. Whitman is always interested in making connections to others in his poetry and prose, although, as I will suggest below, some connections may have been more meaningful than others in Whitman's city. The idea of connection was abstract and material, a real physical desire, and we too often elide the differences between the two. At any rate, Whitman is a significant part of the texture of the notebooks and of Gedney's urban project more broadly.

But there is a further connection that makes the proximity between Whitman and Gedney more pressing still. Among the photographs of New York that Gedney was taking at the time he was keeping the notebooks is a series of Myrtle Avenue. A visual exploration of the kinds of ideas he was jotting down in the Myrtle Avenue notebooks, perhaps. As Geoff Dyer describes it:

> Gedney was fascinated by the history of his street and spent long hours in the local library, excavating its past, transcribing quotations and pasting newspaper accounts of significant events of the street's history into what he designated his 'Myrtle Avenue Notebooks.' Whitman – whose grave Gedney photographed – had also lived on the avenue for a while, and the paper that he had edited for several years, the *Eagle*, boasted that

this first paved and graded street in the area was 'the pride of the old-time Brooklynite.' That was in 1882; by 1939 Henry Miller considered it 'a street not of sorrow, for sorrow would be human and recognizable, but of sheer emptiness.' In the Myrtle Avenue notebooks Gedney uses these two quotations as terminuses between which he shuttles back and forth, preserving the history (through newspaper cuttings) of the street whose contemporary life he was recording in his photographs.[7]

Like Monet's series of London, which captures the city at different times of day, in different light, Gedney's studies capture the different moods of the street, as revealed by the view from his apartment. In part, the series mapped out his personal territory at a time just before the El (elevated train) that he overlooked was scheduled to be demolished. To this extent, there is a kind of cultural preservation at work in his project, an attempt to capture something of the city before it disappears. Permanence and transition rub against each other in the photos, since these are traces of a life and an everyday way of life that was soon to be lost, or at least altered. In 'View of Myrtle Avenue from William Gedney's Window, Brooklyn, 1969', for example, he captures the everyday life of his neighbourhood, as framed by his own personal vantage point. A man dashes for the elevated train – presumably running to the train, but he could equally be running from something we do not see. A woman with groceries pauses in front of a barber's shop. A man, partially out of view, leans on the window in front of a market. A woman walks on the sidewalk. Another man walks on high, on the platform of the elevated train. These are the everyday movements of Myrtle Avenue, each person with his or her own reason for doing whatever it is they are doing, each having his own way of (and reason for) walking, or running, down the street. The photograph doesn't *say* much about these individuals' specific experiences, but it does *show* us something of the collective life of the city: that we often don't know much about what and who we see and that we assume much more than we know about our passers-by.

William Gedney, *View of Myrtle Avenue from William Gedney's Window, Brooklyn,
1969*, photograph.

Whitman's Streets

There is something of the classic urban detective in Gedney's
notebooks – he tracks down his subjects, gathers information and
clues, tries to assemble a plausible reading of his street, past and
present. Whitman is always there, the ghost of a queer neighbour.
That Gedney sought to understand the city through Benjaminian
fragments makes the link between Gedney, the silent observer,
and Walt Whitman, the barbaric yawper, even closer: like Gedney,
Whitman was a great keeper of notebooks, notebooks that reveal
his own explorations of the city. Whitman was perhaps the first
great urbanist in American literature, the first poet of the streets
who found in thoroughfares like Broadway and in the 'profusion
of teeming humanity' an expression of what it meant to be both
modern and democratic, two concepts that are necessarily related
for Whitman. 'After an absence, I am now again (September,
1870) in New York city and Brooklyn, on a few weeks' vacation,'

Whitman writes in 'Democratic Vistas':

> The splendor, picturesqueness, and oceanic amplitude and
> rush of these great cities, the unsurpass'd situation, rivers and
> bay, sparkling sea-tides, costly and lofty new buildings,
> facades of marble and iron, original grandeur and elegance of
> design, with the masses of gay color, the preponderance of
> white and blue, the flags flying, the endless ships, the tumultu-
> ous streets, Broadway, the heavy, low, musical roar, hardly ever
> intermitted, even at night; the jobbers' houses, the rich shops,
> the wharves, the great Central Park, and the Brooklyn Park
> of hills (as I wander among them this beautiful fall weather,
> musing, watching, absorbing) – the assemblages of the cit-
> izens in their groups, conversations, trades, evening amuse-
> ments, or along the by-quarters – these, I say, and the like of
> these, completely satisfy my senses of power, fullness, motion,
> &c., and give me, through such senses and appetites, and
> through my esthetic conscience, a continued exaltation of
> absolute fulfillment.[8]

Whitman was a man of the crowd, someone who loved the city
compulsively. Not only Brooklyn, New York, Camden in New
Jersey, and Washington, DC – the cities he called home – but also
the 'city' as an idea and ideal. Having grown up in rural Long
Island, he was witness to the period of transition from the mid-
to late nineteenth century when New York City transformed
from a relatively provincial city to a cosmopolitan metropolis,
poised to be the definitive city of tomorrow in the first half of the
twentieth century. That sense of futurity appealed to Whitman.
He felt that America's greatness, which is to say, realizing the full
potential of the political mission and cultural output of the young
republic, lay in its future, the exciting possibilities of which were
only suggested in the present. He was always looking ahead, 'For
our New World I consider far less important for what it has done,
or what it is, than for the results to come'.[9] The building of great
cities was one mark of progress, the coexistence of people in a

teeming mass of humanity another, but being able to connect with that teeming mass, to communicate across differences, to touch them, was perhaps the ultimate goal.

It makes sense, then, for Gedney to hark back to Whitman in his notebooks, to revisit and update Whitman's view of Myrtle Avenue and provide a study of the city in movement. And, it makes sense for us to read backwards into Gedney's photos and writing, and end up at Whitman. Both were Brooklynites who lived on the same (but very different) street, and both were tender poets of the streets, in their different media. But the link I wish to make between Whitman and Gedney is more suggestive still, because of the notebooks. Unlike Gedney (or Benjamin), Whitman's notebooks are not cut-and-paste productions, heavy on citation. Rather, Whitman jots things down, records in shorthand fashion things that have occurred, notes autobiographical incidents, and generally philosophizes. This fragment of a poem from sometime before 1860 is indicative of his method and telling of his notebooks:

> *? theme for an immense poem* – collecting, in running list, all the things done in secret.[10]

And that's all. A meagre (fore)shadow of an idea, a quick glimpse into a poem that might have been. The prospect of a poem about secrets is tantalizing, since the only thing more exciting than having one's own secrets is hearing others reveal theirs. There is the promise of revelation in a great Whitman catalogue of names and events, a public outing of secrets and things as yet untold. As it happens, this poem was never written, but the fragment does give us one way to think about Whitman's notebooks, because throughout the pages there are suggestive little traces and fragments that point to, and more or less reveal, a secret life, a private life, the evidence for which remains in lists of fragments and textual traces. Here is only a small selection of names from a long list in a notebook from 1857:

[24] James Gillan (24) driver Myrtle – large country – open faced

Alban Bill (Madison av.) tall black eyed)

Jackson L – (4th av young fellow from Philadelphia

Jack (tallish young Bleecker & 2d st)

?Charley (tallish and goodsized liquid eyed) 4th av – new hand

Charley (East Broadway formerly in Brooklyn

Jack (5th av German birth black eyes & hair 30 now Madison av)

Jo Baker (23) fine head – 4th av

Mike Morrow

Mike – (Bdway) was at Mrs. Hoyts with Dressmaker)

John Brownie – (4th av.) tall, genteel)

? (Jack) Riley

Henry Nelson Hannah

(William (Bdwy) (brother of George, formerly 4th av.) playing ball [:]

Pete (Myrtle and Clermont &c 19 or 20 looks something like George)

Davie – black eyes 25

George Wood (small moustache /

Ike (boy Myrtle) gray eyes) 13 [11]

The full list is several pages long, without much explanation as to why it is there. As the editors of the collected notebooks make clear, lists like these, which are not quite frequent, but are always striking, are something like living proof of Whitman's ideal of 'adhesiveness', his word for male–male love:

> One of the most conspicuous features of the notebooks as they are now published complete is the number of men who are named and briefly identified by appearance or occupation. This list seems to begin in 1856 or 1857, but no doubt they represent a habit of long standing, whether or not records survive. . . . Many of them are totally unidentifiable. Some of them emerge, as one tracks down reiterated names, as people close to him . . . It dawns on one, finally, that whatever other

reasons Whitman may have had for recording all these names, these men had poetic meaning for him, however brief the contact may have been.[12]

Or the lists read like a catalogue of his secrets. It's the poem he never wrote. And I don't think the listings are as mysterious as they first appear. They strike me as (the compulsive) fragments of a cruiser's life, a way to make permanent and less transitory – to record and so to validate – what is essentially and necessarily a fleeting experience of the city, the cruiser's moment of reciprocity. In other of the daybooks and notebooks, the fragments appear to be more explicit, or at least more suggestive:

Dec 28 [1861] – Saturday night Mike Ellis – wandering at the cor of Lexington av. & 32nd St. – took him home to 150 37th street, —— 4th story back room – bitter cold night – works in Stevenson's Carriage factory./

David Wilson – night of Oct. 11, '62, walking up from Middagh – slept with me – works in blacksmith shop in Navy yard – lives in Hampden st. – walks together Sunday afternoon & night – is about 19

Dick Smith – driver 14th St. blonde/

Dan'l Spencer (Spencer, pere, 214 44th St. & 59 William somewhat feminine – 5th av (44) (may 29th) – told me he had never been in a fight and did not drink at all gone in 2d N.Y. Lt Artillery deserted, returned to it slept with me Sept 3d,

Dick Smith blonde, driver 14th St – meet at office every night – at ½ past 8.

James Lennon (Leonard) age 21 Spanish looking – I met on the ferry – night Aug 16 [1879] – lives toward Cooper's Point – learning machinists' trade – 'fond of music, poetry and flowers'[13]

Whitman clearly had an eye for young men, but not all young men; he preferred the men of the streets – policemen, ferry drivers and conductors, working men in general. He met many of the men on the ferry from Brooklyn to New York, or the ferry across the river from Camden, New Jersey to Philadelphia, but also at street corners and on avenues. One of the most important personal and emotionally intense relationships for Whitman was with Peter Doyle, a streetcar conductor whom Whitman met in the 1860s in Washington, DC, when he was living there comforting wounded soldiers. Doyle describes his first meeting with Whitman tenderly:

> You ask where I first met him? It is a curious story. We felt to each other at once. I was a conductor. The night was very stormy, – he had been to see Burroughs before he came down to take the car – the storm was awful. Walt had his blanket – it was thrown round his shoulders – he seemed like an old sea-captain. He was the only passenger, it was a lonely night, so I thought I would go in and talk to him. Something in me made me do it and something in him drew me that way. He used to say there was something in me had the same effect on him. Anyway, I went into the car. We were familiar at once – I put my hand on his knee – we understood. He did not get out at the end of the trip – in fact went all the way back with me.[14]

A lot of energy has been exerted trying to pin down the nature of the relationship between Doyle and Whitman, and between other men close to Whitman throughout his life. Was Doyle his boyfriend? Was he a stand-in for the son Whitman never had? Did their physical relationship extend beyond kissing and cuddling? How can we know? Clearly, their relationship was emotionally intense and probably physically intimate, call it what you will. But suggesting that kind of queer intimacy only gets us so far and may not reveal what some of us wish it to reveal. There is a lot we have to infer about Whitman, much of which comes from the poetry, and there is no explicit letter or other document or piece of 'evidence' that reveals all (in fact, most of Doyle's letters to Whitman do not survive, for whatever reason, which leaves a frustrating silence). There is no smoking gun.

Certainly, attempts have been made to claim Whitman as 'gay', *avant la lettre*. On the one hand, I have sympathy with that move – which is in part to recover the significance of male–male emotional relationships and homosex from the past and to remember and celebrate them – and I appreciate the autobiographical impulse in such a move. I, too, like the idea that there were others before me, particularly others like Whitman. But it is too easy, and even misleading – however self-affirming – to call Whitman 'gay', at least as we think of that term today. In the way I discussed previously, I prefer Neil Bartlett's more ambiguous, tentative, inquisitive and formally more challenging attempt to think about the self through others in the past. In his biography, *Walt Whitman: A Gay Life*, Gary Schmidgall lays claim to the gay Whitman; he says his study is devoted to 'sexual identity, sex, and love' and that he prefers to concentrate on 'the gay Whitman' because 'it is about time': 'Why should we not, by way of ameliorating the imbalance of emphasis at this late date, have something like Whitman the *Gay Lover*, or *Pre-Stonewall Prophet*, or *Bather in Sex*?'[15] Because it is no more accurate that Whitman was 'gay' than it is to suggest that he was straight. I don't wish to appear more hostile than I am to a study like Schmidgall's, but Whitman's challenge is far queerer than the 'gay' or 'straight' (occasionally 'bi') ways of reading him will allow. He is not a figure whose identity we can know through our own categorical terms. Whitman was more radical than that.

Readers of Whitman have always been keenly interested in the 'Calamus' section of *Leaves of Grass*. For those who have sought a 'straight' Whitman, the challenge has been to desexualize Calamus, to interpret his advocation of male 'adhesiveness' alongside his avocation of heterosexual 'amativeness' (found in particular in the 'Children of Adam' section of poems). This reading produces the humanist Whitman, the universalist Whitman. For other readers, the challenge has been 'proving' that Calamus love is the same thing as homosexuality. This produces the 'gay' Whitman. Both readings of Whitman are longstanding and the argument dates back to his contemporaries, for whom defining Whitman was no easy task. The queer reading of Whitman as the poet of sexual radicalism and dissidence – the poet of homosex – can be traced in such writers as John Addington Symonds. He published a study of Whitman in 1893 and was one of those completely taken by what he calls Whitman's 'radical instinct' towards male love and, on a number of occasions, he implored the poet to explain his poems, to elucidate that vision further. In a famous letter to the poet, 'my dear Master', as he calls him, Symonds writes:

> It has not infrequently occurred to me among my English friends to hear your 'Calamus' objected to, as praising and propagating a passionate affection between men, which (in the language of the objectors) has 'a very dangerous side,' and might 'bring people into criminality.'
>
> Now: it is of the utmost importance to me as your disciple, and as one who wants sooner or later to diffuse a further knowledge of your life-philosophy by criticism; it is most important to me to know what you really think about this.
>
> I agree with the objectors I have mentioned that, human nature being what it is, and some men having a strong natural bias toward persons of their own sex, the enthusiasm of 'Calamus' is calculated to encourage ardent and *physical* intimacies.
>
> But I do not agree with them in thinking that such a result would be absolutely prejudicial to Social interests, while I am certain that you are right in expecting a new Chivalry (if I may so speak) from one of the main and hitherto imperfectly developed factors of the human emotional nature. This, I take it, is the spiritual outcome of your doctrine in Calamus.[16]

The invitation to be more explicit about the precise physical nature of Calamus love was one that Whitman declined. In fact, in a famous response to Symonds, Whitman declared that he had fathered six children and was an altogether different sort of man's man. As he got older, he increasingly attempted to set the record straight, by making it look straight, but that didn't really convince Symonds, as a letter from Symonds to J. W. Wallace, one of the founders of the English 'Bolton College' of Whitman enthusiasts, in 1892 makes clear:

> I am still perplexed about the real drift of 'Calamus'. Whitman once wrote me a very emphatic letter, repudiating the idea that under any circumstances the passionate attachment between friend and friend could pass into physical relations. Yet there are certainly a large number of men born with 'homosexual' tendencies, who could not fail, while reading 'Calamus', to think their own emotions justified by Whitman.[17]

In his study of Whitman a year later, Symonds has it both ways: 'Whitman never suggests that comradeship may occasion the development of physical desire. On the other hand, he does not in set terms condemn desires, or warn his disciples against their perils. There is indeed a distinctly sensuous side to his conception of adhesiveness.'[18] He reaches a compromise: homosexuality isn't there, but it isn't *not* there, either. In a pamphlet for the British Society for the Study of Sex Psychology in 1924, Edward Carpenter, a friend of Symonds and another Whitman admirer, suggests that Whitman's less than truthful reply to Symonds was to be expected, since 'no one cares to be pinned down to a state-ment in black and white of his views on a difficult and complex subject'. But Carpenter is no less certain than Symonds about Whitman's particular fondness for men:

> There is no doubt in my mind that Walt Whitman was before all a lover of the Male. His thoughts turned towards Men first

and foremost, and it is not good disguising that fact. A thousand passages from his poems might be quoted in support of that contention – passages in which the male, perfectly naturally and without affectation, figures as the main object of attention, and as the ideal to which his thoughts are directed. These passages are convincing, I think, in their scope, their power and their sincerity. In such a case as that it is useless to rush in with some tag of warning or talk about propriety or morality. What we have to do first is to establish a *fact*, and then afterwards to analyse and discuss that fact; and it seems to me – though of course I may be wrong – that the plain fact is his preoccupation, throughout his poems, with the male rather than with the female.[19]

Carpenter goes on to note something particularly significant, that encountering Whitman's poetry is a turning point in the lives of many men since 'thousands date from the reading of them a new inspiration and an extraordinary access of vitality carrying their activities and energies into new channels.' Where do we go to read about queerness? To Whitman. I don't think we can overestimate the significance of reading and writing, *of books*, in helping queer men to understand that being queer does not equate to being isolated, and this becomes particularly true in the twentieth century.

Xavier Mayne, the author of the touching queer love story entitled *Imre* (1908), privately published a work called *The Intersexes: A History of Semisexualism* (1908), a kind of queer cultural history of Europe, that touches on several great men (and women) of history, a range of fiction, poetry and ancient philosophy, all appropriated for the history and tradition of homosexuality he wishes to tell. As the dedication to Richard von Krafft-Ebing implies, the work is heavily indebted to recent sexological studies; he brings the case-study approach to culture and history in order to discuss homosexual, or 'Uranian', types. There's even a helpful appendix for readers, with numerous questions about homosexuality which assists you in answering the questions: 'Am I at all an Uranian?' – 'Am I at all an Uraniad?'. Unsurprisingly, Whitman is considered 'as one of the prophets and priests of homosexuality':

> One series of Whitman's earlier poetic utterances, at once psychologic and lyric, the famous 'Calamus' group in 'Leaves of Grass', out of dispute stands as among the most openly homosexual matters of the sort, by idealizing . . . man–to–man love, psychic and physical, that modern literature knows; in virility far beyond the verse of Platen; while Whitman much exceeds Platen in giving physical expressiveness to what he sings. Of Whitman's own personal homosexualism there can be no question . . .[20]

In the end, it may not matter whether Whitman was or wasn't homosexual, or whether he intended the Calamus poems to suggest a particular kind of physical encounter. The fact remains that whomever else Whitman may touch, it is undoubtedly the case that he has a particular ability to touch readers who have sex with other men (call us what you will), then and now. I think it is poignant that when someone like William Gedney looks back to Whitman, and makes connections to his own art, it is in part because of such an affinity. Before there were 'friends of Dorothy', there were 'friends of Walt'.

Whitman, like his street-loving European counterpart Baudelaire, was a Bohemian, even at times a dandy. He travelled 'in paths untrodden' for much of his life, as he advocated others to do. Particularly in his youthful prime, he hung out at Pfaff's, a bohemian dive located at 653 Broadway that made its way onto tourist maps of the city and the spirit of which he captures in this poem from a manuscript notebook:

> The vault at Pfaff's where the drinkers and laughers meet to
>   eat and drink and carouse
> While on the walk immediately overhead, pass the myriad feet
>   of Broadway

As the dead in their graves, are underfoot hidden
And the living pass over them, recking not of them, . . .[21]

As he recounted at the end of his life, 'my own greatest pleasure at Pfaff's was to look on – to see, talk little, absorb'.[22] Bohemian life in New York at mid-century was not all about men behaving badly, it wasn't all rakes and libertines, and one of the primary attractions of a place like Pfaff's was its self-consciously 'literary' constituency.[23] It was very much a writer's bar, but it was also very much a man's bar, and Whitman obviously enjoyed both aspects immensely, although perhaps particularly the 'bright eyes of beautiful young men'. Glances, glimpses, stares of one sort or another – all these fleeting ways of seeing were significant for Whitman, who visually consumed the world around him as he loafed about the city or blended into the background at Pfaff's. His many ways of seeing are explored in his journalism and throughout the subsequent editions of *Leaves of Grass*. For example, in a poem such as 'A Broadway Pageant', he sees the city as a panoramic procession, a 'kaleidoscope divine it moves changing before us'.[24] Although different in almost every other way, it reminds us of Wordsworth standing on Westminster Bridge, taking in London with a majestic sweep. A panning shot of the city, but here, peopled and not empty; Whitman lays claim to 'million-footed Manhattan'. 'I will sing you a song of what I behold Libertad', he tells us.[25] That is Whitman, the urban beholder.

But there is another Whitman on the streets, the Whitman revealed in both the fragments in his notebooks and in many of his poems: Whitman the cruiser. In his two-line poem 'To You', he poses a question he returns to a number of times in *Leaves of Grass*:

Stranger, if you passing meet me and desire to speak to me,
    why should you not speak to me?
And why should I not speak to you?[26]

This is a very different sentiment from that we get in Baudelaire. While in a poem like Baudelaire's 'To a Woman Passing By', there is a moment of recognition, it is not a moment imagined as continuing. In fact, the poem we ought to compare with Baudelaire is Whitman's 'To A Stranger':

> Passing stranger! You do not know how longingly I look upon you,
> You must be he I was seeking, or she I was seeking, (it comes to me as of a dream,)
> I have somewhere surely lived a life of joy with you,
> All is recall'd as we flit by each other, fluid, affectionate, chaste, matured,
> You grew up with me, were a boy with me or a girl with me,
> I ate with you and slept with you, your body has become not yours only nor left my body mine only,
> You give me the pleasure of your eyes, face, flesh, as we pass, you take of my beard, breast, hands, in return,
> I am not to speak to you, I am to think of you when I sit alone or wake at night alone,
> I am to wait, I do not doubt I am to meet you again,
> I am to see to it that I do not lose you.[27]

The similarities between Baudelaire's poem and Whitman's are striking. Both eroticize and fantasize about a stranger on the street, both capture the excitement of the passing moment, and both make the temporary permanent through their poems (Whitman also made sure not to 'lose you' by recording his passers-by in his notebooks). But there are differences, too. The speaker in Whitman is very much more a physical presence in the poem – his body becomes an object on display – while Baudelaire's speaker remains distant, can be gleaned only through what he says about the woman passing by.

While Whitman often represents the city in the manner of a *flâneur*, he was as likely to do so in the manner of the cruiser. In other poems, particularly the poems in the 'Calamus' section that celebrate 'adhesiveness' and male love, the street encounter is altogether different, as we see in 'City of Orgies':

City of orgies, walks and joys,
City whom that I have lived and sung in your midst will one
    day make you illustrious,
Not the pageants of you, not your shifting tableaus, your
    spectacles repay me,
Not the interminable rows of your houses, nor the ships at the
    wharves,
Nor the processions in the streets, nor the bright windows
    with good in them,
Nor to converse with learn'd persons, or bear my share in the
    soiree or feast;
Not those, but as I pass, O Manhattan, your frequent and swift
    flash of eyes offering me love,
Offering response to my own – these repay me,
Lovers, continual lovers, only repay me.[28]

Here, Whitman offers an alternative way of experiencing the city, one that replaces the panoramic sweep of 'A Broadway Pageant' with a more personal and individual encounter – an encounter with other men, and quite specifically so given the context of the 'Calamus' poems. This is one of Whitman's great cruising moments, the moment where he offers us a conceptual framework for understanding the self and other in the fleeting moments of the city that does not alienate, does not commodify, does not continue to estrange. On the contrary, the speaker is captivated by the many eyes, the many encounters that reaffirm and 'repay' him. It amounts to a poetics of promiscuity.

Or perhaps we might call it a poetics of reciprocity. As we see frequently in his journalism, and in other poems, Whitman longs for various kinds of connection with humankind. His is a reaching vision that seeks to incorporate everything, to find a language of inclusivity that begins with the self. Whitman as 'kosmos'. But Whitman expresses a language of urban cruising, and his way of representing urban connection becomes the cruiser's way. He seeks to find that other amidst the crowd who returns the glance, that one among many who understands. This becomes clear in another 'Calamus' poem, 'Among the Multitude':

> Among the men and women the multitude,
> I perceive one picking me out by secret and divine signs,
> Acknowledging none else, not parent, wife, husband, brother, child, any nearer than I am,
> Some are baffled, but that one is not – that one knows me.
>
> Ah lover and perfect equal,
> I meant that you should discover me so by faint indirections,
> And I when I meet you mean to discover you by the like in you.[29]

Some are baffled, but one is not. This is what is so liberating about Whitman's vision of the city: it needn't be a place in which individuals remain apart from each other, for each passing stranger is an opportunity to meet that other who understands, who will return the glimpse, and hold your hand, 'speaking little, perhaps not a word'. It relies on the coded behaviour that Whitman somewhat mystically describes as 'secret and divine signs', not unlike the signals Edmund White and Charles Silverstein reveal in *The Joy of Gay Sex* or that we find in the 'psychology of the moment' in Henry Harland's 'A Responsibility'. What is significant in Whitman's cruising vision is that through a kind of learned behaviour of the streets, the modern city is not nearly as alienating as we often presume. Whitman's poetry is, in part, how we learn. He didn't exactly 'invent' cruising as a kind of urban practice, but he imagined it more fully than anyone else had yet done and provided a poetics for the cruiser's way of inhabiting the city.

It may seem obvious to us now that one of Whitman's ways of walking and seeing in the city was also the cruiser's, but it has not always been thus and is still not obvious to all. The cruiser's codes remain uninterpretable to some, or insignificant to others.

What frequently occurs is that the challenging voice of sex radicalism is de-queered in favour of the democratic, individualist
voice of America's National Poet. Whitman is read as a *flâneur*
rather than a cruiser. As I have suggested previously, the *flâneur*
and the cruiser can and often do look a lot alike – they are easily
mistaken – but their aims are different, their conceptualizations of
the city distinct. Dana Brand, in a book on spectatorship in nineteenth-century American literature, says that in Whitman, we
have 'no better example of delighted urban spectatorship'. This is
the Whitman who plunges into the crowd and enjoys the sweeping sights and sounds of the city as pageant and enjoys 'a posture
of detached and delighted omniscience', akin to the narrator in
Poe's 'Man of the Crowd' (who strikes me as far more anxious by
the end, than delighted, but let that pass).[30] For Brand, Whitman
should be read in a long line of *flânerie* writers, which extends
back to Addison and Steele in the eighteenth century and
includes all sorts of (or virtually all) urban writers: Charles Lamb,
Charles Dickens, Pierce Egan and George Reynolds in England;
Poe, George Foster and Hawthorne in America. He sees
Whitman as interrogating the poetics of the 'gaze', but for Brand,
Whitman's gaze is a peculiarly disembodied and abstract one.[31]
The problem is that Brand cannot help but impose a singular,
totalizing way of seeing on Whitman, in terms related to 'the general tendency of the culture of modernity'. Everything must be
made to fit the model of Whitman as detached *flâneur*. The kind
of gazing we get in the 'Calamus' poems – which Brand seeks to
read as 'spiritual' rather than physical, as suggested by Whitman in
the 1876 Preface to *Leaves of Grass* – is a completely desexualized
one: 'As comprehensive as the faculty of sight, "Calamus" love
is a more emotionally charged version of the classic gaze of the
flaneur.'[32] And here is really where he insists too much. He wants
so badly for Whitman to be a 'classic *flâneur*' that he has to explain
too much away and finally doesn't convince. It seems wiser to me
to admit that Whitman writes about walking the streets in many
ways, that he sometimes adopts the pose of the detached 'classic
flâneur', and sometimes adopts the pose (as he did in his own life)

of the sexually interested cruiser, as we see in his poem 'A Glimpse':

> A glimpse through an interstice caught,
> Of a crowd of workmen and drivers in a bar-room around the stove late of a winter night, and I unremark'd seated in a corner,
> Of a youth who loves me and whom I love, silently approaching and seating himself near, that he may hold me by the hand,
> A long while amid the noises of coming and going, or drinking and oath and smutty jest,
> There we two, content, happy in being together, speaking little, perhaps not a word.[33]

Trying to fit Whitman's work into any single conceptual framework is never easy, and to do so risks denying and losing a richer, truly radical vision that Whitman offers: a vision that embraces the multitude and multiple ways of being and seeing. Significantly, in 'A Glimpse', he moves from the *flâneur*'s detached gaze to a human interaction, wordless but touching.[34]

Whitman's reciprocal vision – his queering of modernity – is certainly an idealized vision. It's a model for understanding how we *might* hold the alienating tendencies of modernity at bay. In fact, the radical potential of the cruiser's way of seeing only remains unconventional – even oppositional – as long as we continue to insist on such totalizing visions of modernity as the *flâneur*, a gendered, specific figure if ever there was one. Put another way, if there ever truly *were* an acceptance of the city as a radically fluid and multiple place, then our cruisers, with their secret ways and means, would lose their power to disturb. If the distinction between public and private were ever to break down completely in our urban spaces – in a street, say, or a park, or a toilet – the cruiser would lose his radical edge – he would no longer represent an undermining of totalizing visions. At that point, the cruiser would cease to be queer.

Mapping Manhattan

Whitman was not alone cruising the streets of 'Manahatta'. But how far do the traces of cruising left behind in the notebooks and the glimpses of a city of encounters in his poems get us in understanding the street walking practices of others? Can we talk about a network of cruisers rather than occasional and seemingly isolated, if not accidental, encounters? Whitman's catalogue of men tells its own, personal story of backward glances and reciprocal moments. But it remains difficult to determine the extent of what we might call a 'cruising culture' in New York during Whitman's heyday. What I think it is fair to say is that the ambiguities and uncertain movements that we see occurring in places like Jermyn Street were not unique, either to that street or to London. Clearly, there are significant cultural differences – in streets, as in cities generally – and yet the public spaces of London and New York were marked ambivalently, according to their different uses.

It is still worth asking to what extent was Whitman's cruising part of established cruising patterns and practices that were more or less familiar, at least to those in the know? When he walked the streets, did he do so according to a mental map? How did he know where to go? The ferrymen that Whitman connected with – did others connect, too? The men at Pfaff's – did others see the same kind of beauty in the young men's eyes? Mid-century lower Manhattan and the streets below 14th Street where Whitman loafed were full of drinking dives and brothels, street gangs and violence. It was a raucous and exciting urban scene, and one that Whitman observed up close. The Bowery b'hoys, the roughs and rowdies – he salutes them in his poetry.[35] When Whitman writes about Broadway and about male cruising in the poems and notebooks of the 1850s and '60s, he captures something real about that avenue – its bustle, its overlapping encounters. It is a street where chances might be taken.

I also wonder about the extent to which his poetry might have constructed cruising as a viable street practice for queer men. It is speculative to suggest that we might read – or that others might have read – Whitman's poems quite so *literally*, that readers might have sought out the kind of street encounters described in 'Among the Multitude' or 'A Glimpse', but why not? Whitman's cruising poems are more a call to arms to like-minded comrades than a cruiser's guidebook – a how-to and maybe even a why-to, rather than a where-to. Yet I like to think that some men read 'Calamus' and responded to that call in kind. We all must get our knowledge and construct our map from somewhere.

By the 1890s, when Whitman was a very old man living in New Jersey, the streets he once walked and cruised in New York had become established and well known as queer spaces in which male cruising coexisted, if sometimes uneasily, alongside other ways of experiencing the streets. The Bowery, the centre of prostitution, was also the centre of queer New York, as George Chauncey has documented so fully in his study of *Gay New York*. Paresis Hall, on the Bowery at Fifth Street, was one of the most talked-about queer sites, where the effeminate 'fairies' gathered and made themselves known.[36] Queer lives in the period were not as hidden as we sometimes expect, and queer social scenes were public knowledge and the stuff of gossip. Havelock Ellis, the sexologist whose work on male homosexuality was in many ways so pioneering, speculates in *Sexual Inversion* that in cities, particularly American ones, '99 normal men out of a 100 have been accosted on the streets by inverts, or have among their acquaintances men whom they know to be sexually inverted' – and he notes that all cities have their own networks of meeting places, cafes, churches, clubs and cruising grounds.[37] Queers will always find their spaces in history, however difficult it may be for us to look back and see that now, but by the end of the century in New York, a queer sexual geography of the city had been established (though it continued to shift) and was more or less known by non-queers.

Nowhere is Manhattan's cruising culture in the 1890s more fully and frankly discussed than in Earl Lind's *Autobiography of an Androgyne* (1918). Lind – a self-proclaimed effeminate 'fairy' who also went by the names 'Jennie June' and 'Ralph Werther' – was a male-to-female transsexual, 'a woman whom Nature disguised as a man', as he calls it, castrated in 1898 at the age of 28. The *Autobiography*, most of which was written in 1899, was published in 1918, when he was in his mid-forties, but it documents several years of cruising the streets in the period before his operation. Lind arrived in New York in 1891 as a college student, and not long after he took to the streets. His tendency was to dress down – which is to say, to masquerade and to venture out in disguise – and leave his uptown bourgeois surroundings to go 'slumming' (as he puts it) downtown. But his slumming is more than just the sort of voyeuristic pastime popular with middle-class tourists at the time, and for Lind, slumming veils his cruising. The autobiography is a narrative of extraordinary promiscuity, in which he falls in love a number of times, gets gang raped repeatedly and entrapped in a police sting setting up queers. Frequently it makes for uncomfortable reading, but it is also confirmation of the fluid movement of people like Lind on the streets and of the many kinds of sexual encounters with men.

Like so many books about 'sexual inversion', Lind's account is framed as a sexological case study, prefaced by a doctor testifying to the significance of the patient's narrative for understanding inversion. It concludes with an appendix in the form of a 'Questionnaire on Homosexuality': 'The Medico-Legal Journal, on the basis of the following questionnaire, makes the first essay, in the history of culture, in lining up the defective class in question so that science may have a broader knowledge of them than that afforded by the comparatively few detached biographical and analytical notes at present extant.'[38] It is not strictly accurate to say that this was the 'first essay lining up' the queers – there were other analogous surveys, such as the one found in the appendix to Xavier Mayne's *The Intersexes* mentioned above. But the questionnaire makes its point: that society is trying to make sense of, and find a language in which to discuss, queer sexualities, at least in medical and legal terms. (Society still tries to do this with all expressions of sexuality, all the time.) The questionnaire poses a range of questions that strike us as both amusing but worryingly familiar today: Do you play an instrument? Do you like sports? Do you tend to wear your hair long? Are your sexual organs normal? Do you like loud or fanciful apparel? Answers to questions such as these will apparently help us to know a homosexual when we see him. *Plus ça change.*

The autobiographical account of fairy life in late nineteenth-century New York strikes a familiar chord in other ways, too. Most obviously, *Autobiography of an Androgyne* is a narrative of sexual becoming, charting Lind's years in college and those just after, during which he established what we might now think of as a 'sexual identity' for himself, and found a way of living, however dangerously, that accommodated that emerging identity. 'I longed to be back in a great city', he tells us before his final year in college, 'where alone life is possible for such as me provided one wishes to preserve a good reputation.'[39] Being Earl Lind, or Jennie June or Ralph Werther, or whoever he chose to be, was never particularly easy, but that multiple sense of self was enabled, he suggests, by being in New York, by being in a city where hiding and seeking was routine, and where cruising could masquerade as slumming. Lind's account is also recognizable as a narrative of the country-boy-come-to-town that signals a move from innocence to experience:

> Life in a great city soon made its impress on my constitutional femininity, which, for several years practically suppressed as a matter of conscience, was now calling louder and louder for expression. Moreover, in a great city, the temptation to a double life is exceptional.[40]

Lind's 'great city' is the Anymetropolis of urban modernity and his ways of describing it – as a seducer or temptress who acts upon her citizens – is a common trope. Certainly, the naive outsider who arrives in the city to 'find himself' (or herself, as it happens with the transsexual Lind) is a staple of Anglo-American urban literature, even by the late nineteenth century, and it becomes an outright cliché in the twentieth century. One reason the city is so accommodating for the exploration of identity is that it is a place of doubles, where the individual can be both self and other, where he can become an underground man and go unnoticed and where his secrets can remain secrets. This is, of course, another commonplace of urban literature by this time – we see that most obviously in Poe, Baudelaire, Stevenson and Wilde. Even the queer story of sexual promiscuity – the story of coming rather than becoming, you might say – has its echoes and reverberations. Lind says he had upwards of eight hundred sexual encounters, impressive even by twenty-first-century standards of promiscuity, but it is reminiscent of any number of pornographic picaresques, those sexual adventure stories in which the same scene appears repeatedly in slightly varied forms. Man meets woman, man fucks woman . . . again and again and again. As in a number of late nineteenth-century pornographic works – the mostly heterosexual *My Secret Life* by 'Walter' chief among them, but also Jack Saul's queer narrative in *Sins of the Cities of the Plain* – we may be left asking after reading Earl Lind's account: but is it true? The answer must be, yes and no, because it is narrative, after all. What seems clear is that Lind's account of himself and New York has absorbed a number of narrative conventions in considering the modern city, and for him, the city is an active force, an agent that *creates* certain kinds of behaviour, true to the modern urban sensibility.

Lind's autobiographical account also looks forward to a particular kind of gay male narrative that combines autofictional narrative with promiscuous tales of the streets and bars of queer culture. In the 1950s and '60s there was an explosion in pulp novels, based partly on a formula of sexual conquests in the homosexual 'twilight underworld', which acted as guidebooks to the subcultural scene. 'Hidden within their plots and their characters' lives', Michael Bronski tells us, 'were maps, hints, and clues that told gay men how they might live their lives.'[41] So you might go to a pulp novel in the late 1950s and learn which streets in the Village to walk, which corners in particular to pass, and where to linger. Pulp fiction is different from autobiographical fiction, but forms can act as a guide in revealing the secrets of the city. In recent years, autofiction has been explored fully by Edmund White who celebrates, and turns into high art, promiscuity and cruising of all kinds. *The Farewell Symphony* (1997) is White's sweeping overview of the coming-of-age of a gay writer from the 1960s to the present and the culmination of a series of novels that charts the trajectory of a particular kind of gay man (white, middle-class, American) in the final decades of the end of the twentieth century. Here, sexual promiscuity is at the centre of what gay rights and the liberationist 'Gay is Good' movement are all about:

> We equated sexual freedom with freedom itself. Hadn't the Stonewall Uprising itself been the defense of a cruising place? The newer generation might speak of 'gay culture,' but those of us thirty or older knew the only right we wanted to protect was the right to suck as many cocks as possible. 'Promiscuity' (a word we objected to, since it suggested libertinage, and that we wanted to replace with the neutral word 'adventuring') was something outsiders might imagine would wear thin soon enough. We didn't agree. The fire was in our blood. The more we scratched the more we itched – except we would never have considered our desire a form of moral eczema. For us there was nothing more natural than wandering into a park, a parked truck or a backroom and plundering body after body . . .
>
> . . . If I had sex, say, with an average of three different partners a week from 1962 to 1982 in New York, then that means I fooled around with 3,120 men during my twenty years there. The funny thing is that I always felt deprived, as though all the other fellows must be getting laid more often. A gay shrink once told me that that was the single most common complaint he heard from his patients, even from the real satyrs: they weren't getting as much tail as the next guy.[42]

The right to fuck many people – promiscuity rather than monogamy – was not an agreed right by all gay men who wrote about that particular aspect of some men's experience (see Larry Kramer, for example), and AIDS, of course, tempered the particular narrative thrust that some thought glorified multiple partners as always a good thing. But White was by no means the only one whose autobiographical fictions bring the repetition of multiple partners into play as an organizing narrative principle – in the mid-twentieth century, Jean Genet towers above all others in this regard, but more recent writers including David Wojanorowicz in America and Aldo Busi in Italy also use the stories of the self to address questions of multiple encounters. The French writer Renaud Camus, whose novel *Tricks* (1981) is composed of twenty-five short narratives about male–male encounters, with a preface by no less a cruiser than Roland Barthes, offers us a way to think about the significance of promiscuity. In his brief foreword, Camus suggests that the accumulation of the tricks narrated amounts to an utterance that helps describe the experience of homosexuality: 'Homosexuality, before having a (very hypothetical) *nature*, has a history and, of course, a geography; or in the words of three decades ago, is an *experience* before being an *essence*.'[43] Lind's account of his life and promiscuity documents the cruiser's queer cultural experience; it sheds light on particular aspects of cruising history – transgender ways of living and cross-class encounters – and suggests a very specific queer geography in turn-of-the-century Manhattan.

Like the opening to *Sins of the Cities of the Plain*, Lind's tale of Sodom is a tale of the streets:

> While walking the street, my gaze would be riveted on stalwart adolescents, and I would have to look back at the handsomest that passed. If a street-car conductor happened to be youthful and good-looking, I became almost irrational. With a look of despair I would gaze insolently and imploringly into the face of the blueclad youth as if I would compel him to read my thoughts, since I did not dare give them expression.

When in a crowded car he brushed against me in passing, a tremor would pass over my body. Youthful policemen also at this time particularly fascinated me. Blue clothing and brass buttons have always made a young man appear to me as at his best.[44]

Lind especially likes a man in uniform, and half his eight hundred plus encounters, he says, were with sailors or soldiers. His fetish for rubber boots and military uniforms permeates his life story, and he frequently longs to be a 'fairy', the sailor's word for the man on ship who would act the part of the woman when out at sea. When I read about the streets in the *Autobiography* Whitman is always at the back of my mind – not only because both writers imagine and articulate a culture of cruising (however differently), but also because we know that Whitman's relationship with Peter Doyle began as a conductor/passenger relationship, that they shared a desire to meet working men. In fact, I find the echo of Whitman in Lind's account remarkable, which will strike some people as odd, since Whitman was no fairy, no cross-dresser, no transsexual and, almost certainly, would have disapproved of Lind's effeminacy. The echo is not as explicit as that but exists between the lines. In their different ways, Earl Lind and Whitman share a 'city of orgies, walks and joys', and as I read it, Lind's exploration of the city fills in some of the gaps that Whitman, in his poems and his notebooks, leaves behind.

Lind's nocturnal rambles begin in 1891, in Hell's Kitchen and downtown in the Bowery and, as the narrative progresses, we are given not only a how-to guide for cruising, but also a detailed where-to mapping of the queer sexual geography of Manhattan at the end of the century, the most detailed mapping of downtown cruising I have come across. Here is just one example of Lind's precision pointing (curiously written in the third person):

If the reader had been on Mulberry Street between Grand and Broome on an evening in November of 1892, he would have seen meandering slowly along from one side of the street to the other with a mincing gait, a haggard, tired-looking, short and slender youth between eighteen and nineteen, clad in shabby clothes, and with a skull cap on his head. As he walks along, whenever he meets any robust, well-built young man of about his own age, who is alone, he is seen to stop and address to him a few words. If we had been able to follow this queer-acting individual for the previous hour before he passed us on Mulberry street, we would have seen him roaming about through all the streets of the then dark and criminal 4th Ward, occasionally halting near the groups of ruffians congregated in front of the bar-rooms, and then failing of courage to speak, pass along.

Finally on the corner of Broome and Mulberry Streets, he addresses a tall, muscular, splendid specimen of the adolescent [subsequently a member of the New York police force] who continues in conversation with him, and walks along by his side.[45]

Here, Lind's persona is 'Jennie June', one of the aliases he assumes when cruising, and one that indicates his transgendered sense of himself. Throughout, there is something fascinating about Lind's compulsion to cruise – not least because there is such a compulsive quality to Whitman's poetry and notebooks – but the psychology of compulsion interests me less than the way the cultural and geographical network gets established and known: how does a queer man who wants to meet other queer men *learn* where to go and what to do? In the days before explicit city guides, how did people find out which street to walk or which section of the park to stroll through at night? These questions make the detail with which Lind defines the sexual geography of lower Manhattan all the more striking:

Besides the Bowery, the streets most frequented by me during these nine weeks – as well as during the not immediately fol-lowing two years when I was compelled to go on a female-impersonation spree once in two weeks – were the following: (1) In the foreign Hebrew quarter: Grand, from Bowery eastward to Allen, and Allen and Christie, for several blocks on both sides of Grand. (2) In the foreign Italian quarter, containing also a large sprinkling of Irish immigrants: Grand, from Bowery westward to Sullivan and Thompson; the whole lengths of the two latter streets; Bleecker from Thompson to Carmine; and Mulberry south of Spring. (3) In Chinatown: Doyers, Pell, and Mott streets.[46]

There are other areas of note, particularly in and around the 14th Street theatre district and Union Square where Lind hangs out for a period of months and where the 'young gentlemen libertines' of the middle-classes could be found, but he prefers the ruffians further downtown, where he is more likely to avoid bumping into acquaintances from university and his uptown life.

During his 14th Street days, Lind befriends a group of young adolescents – 'morally and religiously, these young men stood higher than any other class that I ever associated with as "Jennie June"' – who spent their evenings on the park benches in Stuyvesant Square, a few blocks away from Lind's usual haunts:

> The majority of this superior class of young men treated me kindly, but only about one in eight ever went to extremes, and these never more than six times individually. A considerable proportion of those who knew me to be a fairie, however, thought I must therefore be a monster of wickedness, and of the many different sets of adolescents with whom I associated as 'Jennie June,' only one other inflicted on me as much suffering as did this Stuyvesant Square group . . .
>
> . . . They stuck pins into me, inflicted slight burns with lighted matches, and pinched me unmercifully, particularly the penis. There were policemen within hailing distance, but I was told I would be arrested if I called for help. I was entirely innocent, but the police would have believed the false testimony against me of a half-dozen accusers. When satisfied with

wreaking their vengeance, they turned me over to a policeman with charges, but he simply ordered me out of the park.[47]

In recounting this episode, Lind takes the opportunity to argue that the legalization of homosexuality would in no way increase 'homosexual practices' and that being an 'invert' is a victimless crime, 'harmless to society'. But what the Stuyvesant Square episode points to is the constant danger of the streets, even when Lind believes he is in the relative safety of middle-class boys whom he has befriended. A more harrowing story occurs toward the end of an eighteen-month period 'as a Fourteenth Street "street-walker"', when he is picked up and taken back to a young man's room and raped (as always in the *Autobiography*, the explicit descriptions of sexual acts are in Latin, presumably to present the graphic content as discreetly as possible to a target audience of educated men):

> A few minutes after we arrived at the young man's quarters in a furnished-room house, the other five burst in. They proved to be as heartless a gang as I had ever met, although belonging to the prosperous class of society. Misturiverunt super meis vestibus atque me coegerunt facere rem mihi horribilissimam (balneum ani cum lingua, non aliter quammeretrices faciunt). Mecoegerunt recipere tres eodem tempore, fellatio, paedicatio, atque manustupratio. Ultimum mihi imperatum cum adolescens non potuit facere inter femora eodem tempore. Later one who had difficulty in achieving the desired results me coegit ad fellationemunam semihoram continuously, repeatedly punching me in the head and face because I did not do better by him . . .
>
> This was one of my three very worst experiences of sexual abuse. The physical suffering and discomfort were extreme, but I was so fascinated by the savagery and the beauty of my tormentors that I experienced a species of mental satisfaction, being willing to suffer death if only I could contribute to their pleasure. During my career I had numerous experiences, but

much less trying, along this same line. A fairie is often thus treated by cruel, lecherous adolescents, since they know he is an outlaw and cannot bring them to justice.[48]

After yet another brutal attack, Lind reports, matter-of-factly and almost in passing, that 'for two months afterward I suffered pain at every step because of fissures and lacerations about the anus'. While rape and blackmail were everyday possibilities, the threat is worth it because he gets pleasure out of the abuse but, more significantly, the streets also enable him to identify as transgender. On the whole, it is the lower class 'ruffians' who are most accommodating and forgiving of his sexuality, and not his middle-class peers:

> Many a midnight I was promenading the street arm in arm with a pair of adolescent longshoremen cutthroats whom I had never seen before, or with youthful soldiers or sailors. Even some youthful policemen went skylarking with me on the back streets after all the inhabitants had gone to bed. Most of the police on the Bowery knew me as a fairie, but were always friendly. This street at that time was the wide-open 'red-light' district for the un-Americanized laborer and for the common soldier or sailor.[49]

It was during this period, when Lind was more or less living as a woman, that he finds his safest niche, among the working-class immigrants whose own marginal status in American culture may have been one reason for their relative acceptance of Jennie June as part of their street culture. The Bowery emerges as a queerly fluid space that could accommodate difference and the challenges of multiplicity.

Robert K. Martin believes that in Whitman's 'City of Orgies' poem 'his scene of cruising begins the process of creating the modern urban homosexual as an identity. While many of the poems follow a tradition of love poetry that seeks the perfect partner, this poem celebrates another tradition of multiple partners and desires.'[50] Part of Whitman's cruising vision, then, is about finding that one, ideal other in the crowd who glances back, confirming and reciprocating his own erotic gaze. Another part of Whitman's vision suggests a poetics of promiscuity, of the kind seen in 'City of Orgies' or recorded more prosaically in the notebooks. Earl Lind – though he never mentions Whitman in his *Autobiography* – combines both these impulses. His is an ongoing search for the one ideal partner (in his own way), but it is also a reaffirmation of himself through multiple encounters that extend across class and ethnic boundaries and suggests a manner of engagement in which the queer chance encounter represents a significant and important social interaction. As Daniel Altman suggests:

> The willingness to have sex immediately, promiscuously, with people about whom one knows nothing and from whom one demands only physical contact, can be seen as a sort of Whitmanesque democracy, a desire to know and trust other men in a type of brotherhood far removed from the male bonding of rank, hierarchy, and competition that characterizes much of the outside world.[51]

There is no denying that Lind's is a tale of the mean streets, of violence as much as pleasure. But there is also no denying that it is through the streets of the modern city and his many queer encounters with a multitude of men that he is able to realize his own sense of difference. Perhaps this is ultimately what it means to experience freedom in Whitman's cruising democracy.

I met the queer writer Samuel Delaney once, by coincidence at a conference bookstall as I was paying for my copy of Times Square Red, Times Square Blue, *his book about the demise of Times Square porn cinemas. He was standing next to the bookseller when I went up to pay and Delaney asked me whether I would like him to sign my book, and I said yes, I would like that very much, and this is what he wrote:*

To Mark Turner —
Hope you enjoy, possibly even learn, and are reminded of much
Best of the Season —
NYC — MLA
2002
Samuel R. Delaney

I did learn a lot, about Delaney's personal map of the city, his own way of making 'contact' with strangers. I have never been to any of the cinemas Delaney describes, but I have been to others, particularly in Washington, DC, and it was these venues that I was reminded of — of these places and the strangers I have met and with whom I also made contact. Though the city was not the same, the circumstances largely were. Porn cinemas, bathhouses, glory holes, strip joints — they look and act the same in many cities.

The two places I remember best, because I went to them most, were next door to each other on O Street, SE, near the Navy Yard, and practically in the shadow of the Capitol building: the Follies and the Glorious Health club. The Follies was similar to Delaney's porn cinemas, but this one sold sex toys and videos up front and had a dark sex maze through a door on the side of the cinema. It was a friendly place that even offered free coffee in the early hours, although that may have only been for special occasions, like Christmas morning (around 4 or 5 am) when they wanted to lay on something special for those still hanging around. It's not everyone's way to bring in the yule, but it works for some.

The Glorious Health – or Glory Hole as it was popularly known – was adjacent to the Follies (you could move between the two pretty freely, in fact) and it was a no-nonsense, straightforward place that delivered what its name promised many times over – rows and rows of plywood cubicles painted black with holes cut out allowing for easy access to the adjacent cubicles. There's a lot you can do with a big hole in a wall, and there were probably about 40 or 50 cubicles, with open holes in each cubicle, which makes for a lot of holes. It wasn't as clean as the Follies, and made few concessions to trendy décor – its walls had murals in the Tom of Finland style, with decorative graffiti, not to be outdone by the real graffiti in the filthy, doorless toilets. There was a large but solid African-American woman who often worked the door, or window actually, with a baseball bat to hand, in case of trouble. I never saw any trouble though, except maybe once or twice. It was usually quite an amicable place, actually, with a nice mix of men – Catholic boys from Georgetown University, lawyers and lobbyists, tourists, truckers, sailors, marketing men, health workers, retail types, and me and my friends.

As far as I know, the Follies and Glory Hole are still there. Urban regeneration hasn't extended its reach to this part of Washington and, knowing the area, I don't expect it will anytime soon. Compared to Times Square, the real estate isn't so valuable. For years to come, I expect that O Street will continue to provide an important kind of Delaneyan contact.

Chapter Five

Backward Glances at Whitman

Layers of Memory

In 1954, *The Times* published a brief article about a new exhibition of Whitman's manuscripts, letters, books and other items, celebrating his connection to literary friends in England, where he never visited. There is a photo of the iconic Whitman we have come to know best – the old, bearded, rough-and-tumble Walt – looking benignly and sagely at the viewer. Whitman is being honoured by an exhibition at the American Library in Grosvenor Square, being consecrated by the Establishment and getting his due. Directly next to Whitman's story is the headline: 'Lord Montagu on Trial', recording the opening of the trial of Lord Montagu, Michael Pitt-Rivers and Peter Wildeblood who were 'charged jointly and severally with offences arising out of their alleged association with two R.A.F. men, mainly in 1952'. The two airforce men were Edward McNally and John Reynolds:

> The case began in March, 1952, at Piccadilly Circus Underground Station where McNally, on leave from the R.A.F. at Ely, met Wildeblood. They smiled at one another and got in conversation. McNally was taken to Wildeblood's flat in London where, with the concurrence of McNally, unnatural acts were committed mutually between them. McNally was subsequently posted to Blackpool, but returned to London in July when it was alleged that he was introduced by Wildeblood to Lord Montagu, and that subsequently McNally

138

LORD MONTAGU ON TRIAL

THREE MEN JOINTLY CHARGED

FROM OUR SPECIAL CORRESPONDENT

WINCHESTER, MARCH 15

The trial opened before Mr. Justice Ormerod at the Assizes here to-day of LORD MONTAGU of BEAULIEU, aged 27, MICHAEL PITT-RIVERS, aged 36, of Sturminster Newton, Dorset, and PETER WILDEBLOOD, aged 30, journalist, of St. Paul's Road, Canonbury, London. N., who are charged jointly and severally with offences arising out of their alleged association with two R.A.F. men, mainly in 1952.

All three accused were charged together with conspiring to incite the two R.A.F. men, John Reynolds and Edward McNally, to commit unnatural acts and gross indecency. Lord Montagu was charged with attempting to commit a serious offence and acts of gross indecency ; and Wildeblood and Pitt-Rivers were charged with committing serious offences and with acts of gross indecency. There was a total of 18 counts to which all the accused men pleaded Not Guilty.

Mr. G. D. Roberts, Q.C., and Mr. Norman Skelhorn appeared for the prosecution ; Mr. W. A. Fearnley-Whittingstall, Q.C., and Mr. J. Molony for Lord Montagu ; Mr. H. B. H. Hylton-Foster, Q.C., M.P., and Mr. Norman Brodrick for Pitt-Rivers ; and Mr. Peter Rawlinson for Wildeblood.

ACCOMPLICES AS WITNESSES

In his opening statement Mr. Roberts told the jury that they must approach the evidence of Reynolds and McNally with extreme caution. Those men were put forward as perverts, men of the lowest possible moral character, men who were corrupted and, apparently, accepted corruption long before they met the three accused men. It would not be laid at the door of the defendants that they were party to the corruption. These men were witnesses known in law as accomplices ; they were willing parties to these unnatural offences although they were conducted under the influence of lavish hospitality from men who were their social superiors.

It would be highly dangerous to convict any of the defendants on the evidence of either of the two R.A.F. men unless there was confirmation and corroboration from other evidence and outside circumstances of the case. The prosecution hoped to satisfy the jury, from the unusual association of these persons of such social disparity, and from letters and other documents, that there was copious confirmation to prove that Reynolds and McNally were telling a story which, deplorably enough, was true.

BEGAN AT PICCADILLY

LITERARY FRIENDS OF WHITMAN

EXHIBITION IN LONDON

An exhibition of manuscripts, letters, books, and miscellaneous items associated with Walt Whitman was opened yesterday at the American Library in Grosvenor Square, London

The theme underlying the exhibition is Whitman's literary friends. It is, as Mr. Winthrop Aldrich, the American Ambassador, points out in an introduction to the catalogue, a theme particularly appropriate in this country where Whitman had so many admirers. The exhibition comes also at an appropriate time, for 1955 will see the centenary of the printing of *Leaves of Grass*.

The exhibition has been assembled largely through the efforts of Mr. Charles Feinberg, who has drawn on his notable collection and on the generosity of fellow-collectors to bring

A portrait of Walt Whitman, dated 1887.

these books and manuscripts to London. Mr. Feinberg spoke at yesterday's opening ceremony. Walt Whitman, he said, talked for years of travelling to England to visit his friends, but ill-health made this dream an impossibility.

This exhibition was, in some sense, the visit that Walt Whitman had always wanted to make. Its letters, manuscripts, and books were intimately connected with his literary friendships in the British Isles ; among his noteworthy acquaintances through correspondence were Tennyson, Swinburne, Ruskin, Dowden, and Symonds.

BLACKPOOL BRIDGE CONGRESS ENDED

WATER[...] AGAINS[...]

NEGLIGE[...]

A[...]

An allegation [...] patient at Fulha[...] Road, W., was n[...] Division yesterd[...]

Mr. Ernest S[...] Thames waterm[...] Galveston Road, [...] from the Fulham [...] Management Com[...] the hospital in 19[...] Lloyd Temple, re[...] for the use of his left [...] 1948. Mr. Peters [...] of Walton Bridg[...] owners of the Tha[...] he was operating a [...] in an accident in [...] He alleged that th[...]

The management [...] denied negligence [...] that their equipme[...] Mr. Gerald Gar[...] said that Mr. Peter[...] when the brake-ha[...] left arm, and str[...] evening Mr. Tem[...] operation for set[...] Hospital. Mr. Pe[...] of pentothal in his [...] operation it wa[...] anaesthetist injecte[...] artery instead of a [...]

"CRISI[...]

As the effect of [...] the blood there w[...] developing and a [...] Temple recollected [...] what should be do[...] sent for the article[...] the patient was i[...] effect of which [...] coagulant. Counse[...] arm swelled that e[...] removed until anot[...] the next morning [...] once. "Unhappily [...] the damage had b[...]

A further compl[...] the arm was set in [...] a sense the most [...] Mr. Peters was dep[...] obtaining any othe[...] cealed all this fron[...] result is that his har[...] The hearing was [...]

PROPOSED MAIN[...]

LONDON AIR[...]

Adjacent stories in *The Times*, 16 March 1954.

brought a friend, Reynolds, to stay at a beach hut on the Beaulieu estate which was placed at the disposal of Wildeblood and McNally by Lord Montagu, and that offences were committed there. As Lord Montagu was leaving for America, arrangements were made for McNally and Reynolds with Wildeblood and Pitt-Rivers to stay at a house in Dorset, where it was alleged that offences were also committed . . .[1]

In his personal account of the incident, Wildeblood describes his initial meeting more auspiciously: 'I met Eddie McNally on a rainy night in Piccadilly Circus.'[2] I can't help wonder what Walt would have thought of that uneasy juxtaposition: there he is – he who sings the cruiser's song – placed alongside the story of a group of men whose fortunes were determined by a chance encounter at Piccadilly tube station. It is a painfully acute irony to us now, a reminder of the witch hunts of the 1950s, but I am sure it is an irony not lost on at least some readers of *The Times* on 16 March 1954. Wildeblood, Montagu and Pitt-Rivers were each sentenced to eighteen months, while the R.A.F. men were released for having turned Queen's Evidence. The Montagu Trial, as it became known, is perhaps the most well-known gross indecency trial after Oscar Wilde's, although in legal terms it is far more significant as the trial that led to the Wolfenden Committee, whose report in 1957 recommended the legalization of homosexual acts for consenting adults, a recommendation that took another ten years to be passed into law.

Most readers in 1954 wouldn't have known all that we gradually came to know about Whitman, and they almost certainly were not aware of a particularly fascinating part of the notebooks. It wasn't until 1950 that a full 'decoding' of the notebooks revealed the extent of the 'secret and divine signs' in Whitman's private life. In addition to the brief traces documenting the young men Whitman encountered in his everyday life in the city, are still more curious fragments which remained undeciphered until the scholar Oscar Cargill unpacked the riddle of emotionally tortured traces like these, full of underlinings, erasures, different-coloured inks:

July 15 – 1870 –

TO GIVE UP ABSOLUTELY *& for good, from the present hour, this* FEVERISH, FLUCTUATING, *useless* UNDIGNIFIED PURSUIT *of 16.4 – too long, (much too long) persevered in, –* so humiliating *– It must come at last &* had better come now *– (It cannot possibly be a success)* LET THERE FROM THIS HOUR BE NO FALTERING, NO GETTING *at all henceforth,* (NOT ONCE UNDER *any circumstances any circumstances) – avoid seeing her, or meeting her, or any talk or explanations – or* ANY MEETING WHATEVER, FROM THIS HOUR FORTH, FOR LIFE
July 15 '70[3]

Cargill's important uncovering was the meaning of '16.4', the cause of the emotional torment: Whitman's private code for Peter Doyle. The letter 'P' is the sixteenth in the alphabet, the letter 'D' is the fourth, so that '16.4' represents his long-term, off-and-on, male companion. Another scholar, Roger Asselineau, noticed that the 'her' in the first passage above – 'avoid seeing her, or meeting her' – was, in fact, 'him' originally. The 'truth' of the fragment had been erased and rewritten, concealing the identity of the love object and the passion that was the cause of his depression at the time. Later in the notebook, Whitman writes:

Depress the adhesive nature/
It is in excess – making life a torment/[4]

Whitman, in his life and in his work, was full of secrets.

Public Disclosures

Given the kinds of revelations that emerged about Whitman's notebooks, it is no surprise that William Gedney, a gay man who was keenly interested in the emerging gay and lesbian political movements (he photographed its marches and rallies, for example), drew on Whitman in his notebooks and that his work bears the traces of the old visionary poet. It is also not surprising that Gedney was one among many queer artists glancing backwards to

Whitman, only to find Whitman looking forward to him. A few years after the Montagu Trial and a few years before Gedney's Brooklyn series, a young man from Bradford, England went to the Royal College of Art in London, where he almost immediately distinguished himself as one of the most talented artists of his generation. Unlike Peter Wildeblood, who lives on somewhat in infamy, and Gedney, who remains mostly unknown, David Hockney is perhaps the most well-known living British artist in the world today. He is most popularly known, still, for his vibrant paintings of pert, American male buttocks glistening in the turquoise water of LA swimming pools. He has captured like no one else the curious depth of California's sunny surface. But far less considered generally (and known popularly) are his early paintings, from 1960 to 1963 when he was studying in London, when part of his project – part personal, part aesthetic – appears to me to be queerly urban.

Hockney came from Bradford to study at the Royal College of Art in 1959, and the earliest pictures from this time in London show him grappling not only with what every art student at the time had to address – the dominance of abstract expressionism – but also with his own homosexuality.[5] The London Hockney entered was not exactly a 'safe' place for queer men, but it did provide access to others through overlapping social scenes. Describing the queer scene in the persecutory climate of the 1950s, Wildeblood recalls that 'the homosexual world, invisible to almost all who do not live in it, was still as extensive as it had been immediately after the war' and that theatre press nights, private clubs and pubs all provided ways for queer men to socialize queerly in London. But in pubs, in particular, there was also a sense of danger lurking:

> There was always the possibility of a raid. The police did not interfere very much with the clubs, but on one occasion they did swoop on the best-known of them and, examining the membership book, remarked on the fact that most of the clientele appeared to be male. The proprietor coldly replied:

'You might say the same of the Athenaeum. Or, for that matter, of the Police Force.'

The public-houses which had become recognized as meeting-places for homosexuals were less discreet and a good deal more dangerous. With one or two inexplicable exceptions, they were always being raided, and 'warned' by the police.[6]

After the publication of the Wolfenden Report, extreme persecution was less a Home Office and police force strategy than it had been during the witch hunts of the 1950s that led to the Montagu Trial. Still, raids did continue and even as late as the 1980s queer pubs like The Bell in King's Cross were being raided all too regularly. Yet it is fair to say that Hockney arrived in London at a transitional period. In addition to the 1957 Wolfenden Report, which was broadly welcomed by the press and much of the public, in 1958, the Lord Chamberlain removed the ban on plays addressing homosexuality, resulting in a new wave of queer representation (Geoff in Shelagh Delaney's *A Taste of Honey* in 1960, for example) and the Homosexual Law Reform Society was organized in 1960 to push for the decriminalization of homosexuality.[7] The times were slowly changing, in the metropolis at least, and the early 1960s could be an accommodating time to be queer in London for many artists and others. Writing specifically about Hockney, Paul Melia has reminded us that, 'By the early sixties, London enjoyed a network of meeting places for homosexuals: pubs, private clubs, public toilets and parks. During 1959–60, his first year at the Royal College of Art, this variegated subculture provided Hockney with a source of social support and information; during 1960–61, it became the subject for his practice.'[8] It is the move from initiate in the above and below ground queer scenes to queer experience as subject matter in his artistic practice that interests me.

Even in his early more abstract paintings, before he developed the colourful style that defines his work in America, Hockney was moving to address 'personal' subject matter publicly in his paintings and to find a way to integrate his inclination toward

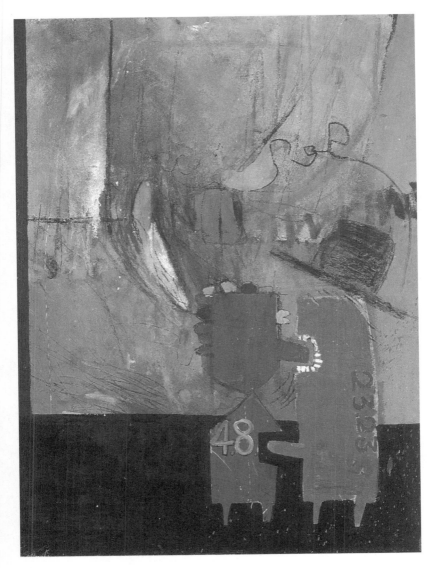

David Hockney, *Adhesiveness*, 1960, oil on board.

figurative representation with abstraction. In paintings like *Erection, My Carol for Comrades and Lovers, Going to be Queen for Tonight* and *Queer*, Hockney essentially deals in the abstract, but uses words and phrases to suggest possible sexual and erotic meanings. He becomes less suggestive and more specific when he paints *Adhesiveness* in 1960. As a number of art historians have observed, the painting figures as part of a series that explores figuration as opposed to abstraction and engages with the visual language of homosexuality. *Adhesiveness* was the most sexually explicit painting he had yet produced, and it is also the painting with the first direct reference to Walt Whitman. No coincidence, that.

Hockney's use of Whitman is twofold in the picture – firstly, he borrows Whitman's very particular term for male comradeship and love, his Calamus ideal, and, secondly, he incorporates Whitman's numerical code for documenting young men that he met on the streets of the city, the code that was broken in 1950. His is a very specific appropriation of Whitman, then, that points directly to the ambiguous overlap between the ideas explored in the poetry (in particular, male love and its link to democracy) and the private way Whitman documented his own relationships with men. Hockney's appropriation of Whitman makes ridiculous the kind of silence about queerness that could exist on the page of *The Times* during the Montagu Trial and the kind of erasure of queerness that we find in some critical readings of Whitman. For Hockney, Whitman's sexuality – and the way he expressed and represented it – mattered.

Adhesiveness is a painting that in part allows him to explore that aspect of himself, as he records:

> It was my first attempt at a double portrait. I also used Whitman's rather childish little thing about playing with each letter of the alphabet . . . so the painting has these code numbers on it. I like the idea of putting numbers and letter-ing on it in just the same way the cubists put numbers on their work. The numbers really say 'DH' and 'WW'. I

remember in the summer of 1960 I read everything by Walt Whitman . . .[9]

The use of seemingly random bits of text suggests the fragment-ed approach to urban modernity that we have seen in so many who engage with the city, and cubist painters no doubt figure largely in the back of Hockney's mind but, tellingly, Whitman's code gives the painting a kind of coherence. It makes sense of what would otherwise be simply undecipherable traces. In a slightly later painting, *Doll Boy* (1960–61), Hockney encodes the popstar pin-up Cliff Richard's name – 3.18 – in a painting whose title refers to Richard's hit single 'Living Doll', and which also incorporates the words 'Queen' and 'Doll Boy', making explicit his queer use of Whitman's code. There is a longing for something Hockney knows he cannot have, but it's not the tor-turous and 'humiliating' longing of Whitman for Peter Doyle. Hockney turns Whitman's shame on its head in his playful appropriation.

There are a number of reasons Hockney might have looked to Whitman. His own personal reading, as he suggests, is one. But he was in a tradition of queer men who looked back to Whitman as their intellectual, artistic and emotional guide. In addition to those in his own day like Symonds and Carpenter and other enthusiasts, Whitman had had an impact on a generation of queer avant-garde American artists in the early twentieth century, par-ticularly figures such as Marsden Hartley, whose painting of Whitman's house in Camden is a kind of homage to the radical poet. Jonathan Weinberg believes that 'painting Whitman's house was a way to connect with the dead poet, whose work was important for Hartley, not just for its expression of homosexu-ality but for its attempt to make a marginalized experience central to the culture'.[10] What a painter like Hartley found in Whitman was a fusion of queer radical concerns and something like the national spirit (call it democracy, for the sake of argument). Whitman looked to the margins and made them central, which clearly appealed to those who felt marginalized.

Furthermore, in celebrating Whitman, Hockney was doing what so many others were doing at the time, especially in America. 'Whitman's excesses,' Michael Davidson writes, 'so embarrassing to an earlier generation, became his virtues for poets who came of literary age in the 1950s and 1960s. His direct address, sexual themes, and open forms offered a salutary alternative to literary and social formalisms.'[11] The ghost of Whitman haunted a whole range of radical, alternative and queer urban writers, two of whom I'll single out, Allen Ginsberg (the Beat) and Frank O'Hara (the camp and wry ironist). For Ginsberg, it was Whitman's ideal of adhesiveness that appealed, for the way it suggested tender communication between people that extended beyond the marketplace, beyond America's impulse to unite through incorporation. Ginsberg's sexual frankness, his pursuit of spiritual awareness through physical pleasure and bodily exploration, his love of men, and his freewheeling verse form – all owe a debt to Whitman. In his call-to-arms, *Howl* (1956), he sings the song of his generation, for those

who let themselves be fucked in the ass by saintly motorcyclists, and screamed with joy,

and for those

who hiccupped endlessly trying to giggle but wound up with a sob behind a partition in a Turkish Bath when the blonde & naked angel came to pierce them with a sword . . .[12]

These are Ginsberg's Whitmanesque multitude.[13] By contrast, Frank O'Hara glances back to Whitman in other ways, in particular through his depiction of the city, its streets, its cruising. Neil Bowers believes O'Hara's poetry is 'the culmination of the Modernist poetic urbanization represented by Whitman, Williams, Eliot and Crane'.[14] According to his biographer Brad Gooch, O'Hara – like other contemporary poets and artists – was 'trying to create a poetic city of New York', and his poetry over the

course of his short life amounts to what Gooch calls 'a fragmented epic of the city'.[15] This suggests that in order to get a complete
understanding of O'Hara's vision of the city, you have to read *all*
the poetry, rather than a single poem – his vision is accumulative,
with many different kinds of glimpses, encounters and points of
view, very much in the manner of Whitman. Individual poems do
reveal telling connections to Whitman, particularly in O'Hara's use
of cruising, far more sexually explicit than Whitman's but offering
similar kinds of connection in the city. '[I]t's the night like I love
it all cruisy and nelly', he writes in 'Easter', and so it was in his personal life.[16] Streets, parks, toilets in subway stations, docks – all
these were markers on O'Hara's sexual map of the city that he
explored with relish.[17] He would go cruising during his lunch
hour, after work, at night, and was fairly open, at least with some
friends, about his multiple partners. His poem 'Homosexuality'
(written in 1954, although not published until 1970) begins, with
an unveiling – 'So we are taking off our masks, are we, and keeping / our mouths shut? As if we'd been pierced by a glance' – that
later leads us to 'the merits of each / of the latrines. 14th Street
is drunken and credulous, / 53rd tries to tremble but is too at
rest . . .'.[18] Like so many of O'Hara's poems, 'Homosexuality' is
pointed and ironic, in part a jab at queeny homosexuals, but it is
also the work of a keen cruiser who knows the various scenes
well.

Hockney couldn't have been familiar with a poem like
O'Hara's 'Homosexuality', because it hadn't yet been published,
but that isn't really the point. That Hockney should look back to
Whitman and revise his vision of the city and urban encounters
was in keeping with the spirit of the times, particularly in
America. Hockney may not have been the first to use Whitman
as a way into thinking about the representation of sexuality visually, but he is one of the most open in adopting Whitman's queer
code as part of his own representational language. Furthermore,
the manner of his engagement – not just that he engages – in *The
Third Love Painting* (1960) is particularly striking since the canvas
is covered with graffiti, most of which, Hockney tells us, comes

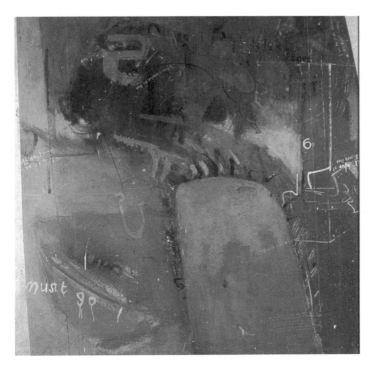

David Hockney, *The Third Love Painting*, 1960, oil on board.

from things he had seen written on the toilet walls at Earls Court Underground. The graffiti draws the reader in to the painting – 'You want to read it', he says – but the graffiti also blurs the boundary between Whitman's poetry and the poetic scrawls of everyday life: 'When you first look casually at the graffiti on a wall, you don't see all the smaller messages; you see the large ones first and only if you lean over and look more closely do you get the smaller, more neurotic ones.'[19]

Hockney's brilliant gesture is to take Whitman's lines from 'When I Heard at the Close of Day' and present them as graffiti, alongside the 'real' graffiti represented on the canvas: 'Britain's future is in your hands', 'Ring me anytime at my home' and 'come on David admit it'. It's a confrontational move in the sense that he challenges the viewer by making him look more closely at the canvas, making him question what he's seeing and reading, and how he is supposed to interpret it. Hockney's use of graffiti also echoes other city painters for whom the use of graffiti was an expression of the fragmented nature of urban modernity, with its own undecipherable writing on the wall – artists such as George Grosz, whose drawings and paintings of Berlin frequently include scratchings of graffiti. Graffiti is in some ways the most democratic of our urban arts, even while it has a long and distinguished history of being appropriated in high art, but it's also an artistic practice that remains illegal. To write graffiti is to make one's individual mark in public space through vandalism, to commit a crime – even if that public space may appear to be the less public and more private space of the tube station toilet (it depends on who's using it and how). Derek Jarman suggests that

> graffiti are the scratchy attempts by the sexually imprisoned to liberate themselves. They are pathetic remnants of a lost language of love, condemned to the walls of the toilet.
> Graffiti, stammerings, they are always man to man.[20]

Thought about in this way, Hockney's graffitization of the poet makes Whitman's lines a kind of 'lost language', which he builds into the layered visual language of his paintings. Hockney takes Whitman, the great vandal of poetic form and subversive cruiser of the streets of the metropolis, and puts him where he belongs: in the toilet. It doesn't get much more democratic than that.

There are a number of ties that bind the cruiser and the writer of graffiti – the subcultural claiming of public spaces; the fact that the cruiser and graffitist are both around but often are not detected committing their crimes; their use of anonymity; and, the coded use of private languages. Part of the effectiveness of graffiti comes from its being indecipherable, a language from which most of us are excluded. Its confrontational utterance graphically forces itself on you – it often demands attention – while at the same time excludes you from its own secret codes. The public inscribes the private; some can interpret the writing on the wall, but by no means all or even most of us. Furthermore, graffiti on the walls of the city (its buildings or its loos) acts as an extended conversation – sometimes between strangers, sometimes not. Graffiti writers leave messages for others; they delete by writing over previous textual traces; and they exchange information. On the wall of a toilet stall, that exchange of information may be a phone number or proposition but it is no less conversational because of that.[21] In a way, Hockney turns Whitman into a graffiti writer whose very public lines of poetry are linked to a very private, even subcultural language (in the notebooks) that only some could read, but a public gesture nonetheless. 'Some are baffled, but that one is not – that one knows me', writes Whitman of the city in 'Among the Multitude'. It's a way of conversing and representing a form of contact, and one that entails social interaction every bit as much as other more 'respectable' forms of contact.

In his recent book *Times Square Red, Times Square Blue* novelist and critic Samuel Delaney discusses the recent 'regeneration' of Times Square in New York which altered it from being the centre of the porn cinema industry to the corporate and Disneyfied entertainment complex environment that it is today. It is really two long essays, the first a very personal and anecdotal account of the porn cinema culture he frequented for about 30 years; here, he talks about the significance of the relationships he had with many different men over the years, in the cinemas and on the streets outside—the hustlers, the homeless, the insurance salesmen, the lawyers, the working-class labourers, the neighbourhood shoe-shine, the hotdog vendor – the various men whose paths crossed, however briefly, in the hazy light of big-screen pornographic films. The second essay is a more theoretical discussion of the kinds of issues raised in his personal memoir of Times Square, and, in particular, Delaney reflects on the significance of those chance sexual encounters that he sees as a vital form of social contact in the city:

Contact is the conversation that starts in the line at the grocery counter with the person behind you while the clerk is changing the paper roll in the cash register. It is the pleasantries exchanged with a neighbor who has brought her chair out to take some air on the stoop. It is the discussion that begins with the person next to you at a bar. It can be the conversation that starts with any number of semiofficials or service persons – mailman, policeman, librarian, store clerk or counter person. As well, it can be two men watching each other masturbating in adjacent urinals of a public john – an encounter that, later, may or may not become a conversation. Very importantly, contact is also the intercourse – physical and conversational – that blooms in and as 'casual sex' in public rest rooms, sex movies, public parks, singles bars, and sex clubs, on street corners with heavy hustling traffic, and in the adjoining motels or the apartments of one or another participant, from which nonsexual friendships and/or acquaintances lasting for decades or a lifetime may spring, not to mention the conversation of a john with a prostitute or hustler encountered on one or another street corner or in a bar – a relation that, a decade later, has devolved into a smile or a nod, even when (to quote Swinburne) 'You have forgotten my kisses,/And I have forgotten your name.'[22]

Contact as Delaney means it often appears to us as the small stuff of our everyday lives. But the accumulation of the small stuff – all those little traces brought together, all those exchanges on the street, the 'hello's and the smiles, the random meetings here and there – this is part of the fabric of our social lives in the city. Delaney's encounters, when he looks back on them, are perhaps more significant than they seemed at the time, because they always lead us somewhere else, but in particular to others:

They were encounters whose most important aspect was that mutual pleasure was exchanged – an aspect that, yes, colored all their other aspects, but that did not involve any sort of life commitment. Most were affable but brief because, beyond pleasure, these were people you had little in common with. Yet what greater field and force than pleasure can human beings share? More than half were single encounters. But some lasted over weeks; others for months; still others went on a couple of years. And enough endured a decade or more to give them their own flavor, form, and characteristic aspects. You learned something about these people (though not necessarily their name, or where they lived, or what their job or income was); and they learned something about you. The relationships were not (necessarily) consecutive. They braided. They interwove. They were simultaneous.[23]

The messages of graffiti — wiped out, overwritten, added to, extended — on a toilet cubicle wall are evidence of — no, an affirmation of — the overlapping, non-consecutive, interwoven contact that goes on all around us, all the time. They are traces of that contact. By reimagining and updating Whitman, Hockney enters another kind of conversation and puts us into contact with Whitman and the culture of his streets by bringing the past to bear on the present, and in so doing, he also realigns Whitman as the poet of cottaging, the poet of contact.

Another of the graffiti paintings, Hockney's *We Two Boys Together Clinging* (1961), borrows its title from the following poem by Whitman:

> We two boys together clinging,
> One the other never leaving,
> Up and down the roads going, North and South excursions
>   making,
> Power enjoying, elbows stretching, fingers clutching,
> Arm'd and fearless, eating, drinking, sleeping, loving,
> No law less than ourselves owning, sailing, soldiering,
>   thieving, threatening,
> Misers, menials, priests alarming, air breathing, water drinking,
>   on the turf or the sea-beach dancing,

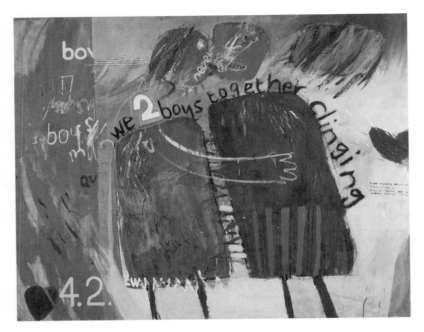

David Hockney, *We Two Boys Together Clinging*, 1961, oil on board.

> Cities wrenching, ease scorning, statutes mocking, feebleness
>   chasing,
> Fulfilling our foray.[24]

Hockney includes the first line, and bits of lines three and four. The word 'never' is between the faces of the two figures – suggesting a double meaning, as in 'never' to be, indicating that Whitman's ideal is still a utopian one, but perhaps also pointing to 'never leaving' as in line two of the poem. He also publicizes Whitman's private code again, with '4.2' again referring to 'Doll Boy,' which links this painting back to *Doll Boy*. The clingingness is a feature of the paintwork, but it probably also refers to Whitman's adhesiveness, represented very physically in the poem by the 'clinging' and 'clutching' of the two boys' bodies. Hockney says of *We Two Boys Together Clinging*:

The emphasis in the painting is on 'clinging'; not only are the arms clinging but small tentacles help keep the bodies close together as well. At the time of the painting I had a newspaper clipping on the wall with the headline 'TWO BOYS CLING TO CLIFF ALL NIGHT'. There were also a few pictures of Cliff Richard pinned up nearby, although the headline was actually referring to a Bank Holiday mountaineering accident. What one must remember about some of these pictures is that they were partly propaganda of something I felt hadn't been propagandised, especially among students, as a subject: homosexuality. I felt it should be done. Nobody else would use it as a subject, but because it was a part of me it was a subject that I could treat humorously. I love the line, 'We two boys together clinging'; it's a marvellous, beautiful, poetic line.[25]

For Hockney, referring to Whitman was one of the ways that he could publicize homosexuality, and his own sexuality, in London. He makes public Whitman's private language and makes explicit the implications of his cruiser's vision of contact with other men, and in so doing, Hockney makes his own private life public.

The political significance of this gesture – his relaxed, what-about-it attitude to homosexuality – should not be underestimated, for as Derek Jarman notes, it was Hockney and painting (rather than other art forms) that made queer representation public:

The theatre reduced us to a load of laughable pantomime drag queens; it was in painting that the leap forward into normality was made in *We Two Boys Together Clinging* by David Hockney, and later the startling reality of lads I knew or recognized in bed together in the *Cavafy Etchings*.[26]

Hockney merges his life with the queer lives of those who came before him, men like Whitman and Cavafy, appropriating them as necessary to make his own point. It isn't so far from Bartlett's strategy in taking on Wilde. Both are acts of queer revisionism, nothing as simple as homage, and both bring to light the footnotes of history, the scratchings at the margins of mainstream experience. In his journals, David Wojnarowicz, the queer writer and artist whose anger at America in the 1980s echoes Ginsberg's *Howl* (echoing Whitman) attests to the significance of publicizing the private:

> To make the *private* into something *public* is an action that has terrific repercussions in the preinvented world. The government has the job of maintaining the day-to-day illusion of the ONE-TRIBE-NATION. Each public disclosure of a private reality becomes something of a magnet that can attract others with a similar frame of reference; thus each public disclosure of a fragment of private reality serves as a dismantling too against the illusion of ONE-TRIBE-NATION; it lifts the curtains for a brief peek and reveals the probable existence of literally millions of tribes.[27]

Hockney's gesture in using Whitman is part of a dismantling of the institutions of the Establishment – Wojnarowicz's ONE-TRIBE-NATION – an expression of private difference made public. Indeed, there's a bravery in Hockney's move (as there is in, say, Peter Wildeblood's autobiography), in being openly queer in this way – a bravery resonant of the kinds of contact Whitman dares to express in his 1860 Calamus poems, a kind of militancy similar to that of the urban graffiti artist who claims his own territory and inscribes his own space in public.

While the series of pictures he creates in 1960–61 in those heady, exploratory years as a student in London may seem very different from his later work, there are continuities worth noting. First, because Hockney remained an artist of the streets, and continued to be inspired by the traces of homosex culture he came across. A line from Auden's *Homage to Clio* is rewritten in *The Fourth Love Painting* (1961) to suggest a random encounter in a toilet; John Rechy's novel about hustlers and queer urban life, *City of Night*, informs Hockney's vision of *Building, Pershing Square, Los Angeles* (1964); and the beefcake magazine *Physique*

Pictorial led him to begin painting those wonderful, pert, pink American bottoms he liked so much.[28] Second, he remained interested in representing the possibilities of the street encounter, even if he himself was not promiscuous most of the time. As Andrew Causey describes it, a painting such as *Santa Monica Boulevard* (1978–80) 'was Hockney's attempt to create a kind of living city, a theatre of the everyday', with its depiction of hustlers and cruisers alongside other passers-by.[29] Even if the scratchy, rubbed-out, written through, urban terrorist-style graffiti aesthetic that he explores in the defining moment of 'becoming Hockney', the artist and the sexual being, never really emerges again in his paintings (it does remain to an extent in his etchings), he continues to connect his life to other lives, to other experiences, to buildings and streets that ostensibly have nothing to do with him. In this sense, like Neil Bartlett and others, Hockney imagines a kind of transformation – one that asks us to examine traces, to look closely and pay attention to the alternative meanings of the writing on the wall.

And what of Whitman? The appropriations, revisions, and re-readings continue, long after Hockney and Gedney in the 1960s. Entire anthologies are devoted to his legacy, his afterlife. We're still very much in contact with his city of men. As the contemporary American poet Mark Doty writes,

> all century, poets lining up
> to claim lineage. And not just poets –
> in a photobook, brand-new,
> handsome lads wrestle in sepia,
>
> freshly laved by some historic stream:
> the roughs are models now, and pose
> in nothing on the opposite pages from stanzas
> of your verse: a twentieth-century
>
> letter to you. As are the scrawls
> beneath the underpass, ruby and golden

cuneiform reinscribed on train-car sides:
songs of me and my troops, spray-painted

to our prophet, who enjoins us to follow . . .[30]

Doty's poem recounts a pilgrimage he makes to Camden, New Jersey, to see the house where Whitman lived. It is a kind of homage, similar to Marsden Hartley's, perhaps, and a visit similar to one many queer men make every year; but Doty also considers the fate of Whitman's America (that is, in 1997 when the poem first appeared), the fate of his optimism for the future greatness of democracy. What he finds is that Camden at the end of the twentieth century bears all the hallmarks of the abandoned inner city, 'Jail, detox, welfare', while middle-class citizens like Doty are part of a different crowd in the shopping centres and parking lots across America. In this way, the poem can be read as a lament for Whitman's modern urban vision and for his emphasis on the greatness of America's future. Doty is also keenly aware of all the appropriations of Whitman – all the poets (some of whom I have mentioned already) and that 'photobook', which happens to be David Groff and Richard Berman's photo-illustrated book of Calamus extracts, *Whitman's Men*. But there was another photobook published in 1996, Duane Michals's *Salute, Walt Whitman*, that similarly juxtaposes lines from Whitman with contemporary photos. Michals's vision of Whitman – like many others' – is a rural, wilderness vision – it's an interpretation that abandons the city. Like Groff and Berman's book, beautiful, muscled bodies stare out at the viewer or hold copies of volumes with Whitman's lines inscribed on their pages, although the images are less about the body and sexual acts than they are about comradeship and the ideal of adhesiveness. His comrades and boys together clinging exist completely apart from the urban centres, away from the bustle of modernity, out of the crowd, in another kind of ideal America, another kind of ideal that we, too, find in Whitman. It is telling partly because Michals is a photographer who, elsewhere, is interested in precisely the random encounters with strangers that are so significant in Whitman's poetry. In his work 'Chance Meeting' (1970), a series of photographs that depict two men passing each other in an alley, both looking back to see the other, Michals explores exactly the kind of chance encounter one imagines in Whitman's 'A Glimpse' or 'Among the Multitude', and for Michals it was a gesture at exploring his own gay sexuality. But for whatever reason, in his salute to Whitman, it was the rural rather than the urban poet he chose to salute, the 'open road' of America he chose to romanticize.[31] In Doty's 'Letter to Whitman', the allusion to the photobook is part of the route that leads back to Whitman's home in Camden, but the graffiti he passes along the way offers a more difficult and uncertain reading of the city than it does in Hockney's paintings. For Hockney, the transformation of Whitman's poetry into graffiti is part of a self-exploration, a provocatively public display of sexuality and also an updating of the queer cultural history of the city. For Doty, the graffiti is more ambivalent, it leads back to Whitman but it also measures, perhaps, just how far we now are from the cruiser's vision of a democracy of contact with strangers in the streets of modernity.

centralhornyguy:	*hey whats up*
irishlndn:	*not much, yet :-) u?*
centralhornyguy:	*lol. yeah, same. bored, killing time. no wait, MURDERING time. oh and horny. where u?*
irishlndn:	*lol. nr waterloo. what u looking for?*
centralhornyguy:	*depends. maybe a meet? am not too far from waterloo*
irishlndn:	*u got a pic?*
centralhornyguy:	*no . . . usually do, but it's on a disk at home, and am in my office. u?*
irishlndn:	*only to swap. stats?*
centralhornyguy:	*5.11, br hair/eyes, avg build (go to gym tho), good looking (i would say that), 7 cut, clean shaven, some hair on chest*
irishlndn:	*sounds nice. what u into?*
centralhornyguy:	*stats?*
centralhornyguy:	*nothing too heavy . . . just some horny fun, whatever*
irishlndn:	*hang on, will message u my pic*

centralhornyguy:	*cool, thnks. what u into?*
irishlndn:	*a meet would be good. u str8 a/l?*
centralhornyguy:	*hey nice pic. cute! yeah, totally str8 acting*
centralhornyguy:	*u there?*
centralhornyguy:	*HELLO*
centralhornyguy:	*??????????*
irishlndn:	*back. sorry. phone.*
centralhornyguy:	*no prob. u must be popular. anyway . . .*
irishlndn:	*so u like to suck? how old u?*
centralhornyguy:	*yup. 30. u? where u live?*
irishlndn:	*south, but cant accom. am 26*
centralhornyguy:	*u look younger. i can accom :-)*
irishlndn:	*usu dont meet w/out pics. but am really horny! LOL*
centralhornyguy:	*me too. ring me, here's my mobile . . .*

Epilogue

Cruisingforsex

Cruising the streets of our cities isn't what it used to be. The 'secret and divine signs' that Whitman imagined in urban encounters still allow men to connect, but circumstances have changed, our cities have changed and our understanding of sexualities has changed. Nowhere has the transformation of cruising practices been more obvious than in the world of cyberspace. The lure of cybercruising has radically altered what it means to cruise and how we go about it. When we think about cruising today, a much broader range of social practices comes to mind, and these are not necessarily urban – truck stops, toilets in various locations, highway rest areas, parks, cinemas, adult bookstores. All of these provide opportunities for men to meet and have sex with other men, as they have done for a long time, but the internet is now a key medium through which real meetings in these places occurs. But what happens to the cruiser once he leaves the network of streets, parks, toilets and other urban places and enters the network of virtual locations that is cyberspace? What is the psychology of the virtual moment of contact? What relevance is geography in a global cyberspace that appears to challenge the very notion of borders and boundaries? The internet enables a range of different kinds of interactions, and all these questions suggest that whatever cruising might be and mean in the twenty-first century, it is different from the kinds of exchanges that took place on Jermyn Street or in Stuyvesant Square.

Cruising on the web takes many forms, and offers a range of interactions. There are things like university cruising groups that facilitate sex meets on campuses; Yahoo email members' groups such as LondonQuickie put cruisers in contact with other cruisers for lunchtime rendezvous in the city centre; chatrooms allow users the opportunity to engage with others in the same virtual space at the same time by exchanging messages in real time (and/or watching each other via webcams, for those technologically advanced enough). Still other sites act, at least in part, as clearinghouses, providing vast amounts of information on cruising grounds and practices around the world and also enabling cruisers to interact through chatrooms and message boards – websites such as *squirt.com*, *cruisinground.com* and, the most successful of them all, *cruisingforsex.com*.

Cruisingforsex.com (or CFS, as it brands itself on t-shirts, coffee mugs and sundry other items for sale on the site) offers an ever-increasing array of features and options for the user (presumably a man) interested in sex with other men. What started out as a small cottage industry, with a listing of places where men could cruise and meet for sex, across America and beyond, has turned into a denser, more layered and more far-reaching site. In addition to the sex listings, which are still a major attraction, there's a message board, a cruiser's photo gallery, a 'cruiser of the week' featuring a 'real' user, a chatroom (in which almost no one ever chats). Regular, more discursive features include porn video news and reviews, the 'guidance counsellor' advice column (much of which is related to sexual health), escort reviews and city reports from New York, Vancouver, Seattle, London and a couple of other English-speaking cities. There's no doubting the popularity of CFS, and as it advertises on the homepage, it is 'ranked in the top 1.2 percent of ALL websites for traffic, with over 1,500,000 visitors cruising by each month'. Keith – the site's founding 'cruisemaster' and its full-time minder – suggests in his welcome section that:

The cruisingforsex.com Website is dedicated to helping men around the world connect for sexual pleasure. You will need a healthy attitude about your sexuality to fully enjoy my site.

Leave your guilt at the door, please. Most of my site visitors are gay or bisexual men, but a large number are straight (not bi) guys who recognize the satisfaction that can be had from sexual release with a guy from time to time.[1]

Unlike other kinds of cruising sites – in particular, chatrooms such as *gaydar.com* or *gay.com*, CFS makes a point of noting that having sex with other men is not a gay practice alone, that many straight-identified men use the site to get in touch with other men, virtually and in person. For the beginner cruiser, Keith provides a brief etiquette guide to cruising, called 'Cruising 101: Skills for Safer, Successful Cruising'. 'Use common sense', he tells us. 'The key to keeping public sex alive and well in your favorite place is to conduct yourself using common sense and civility towards other cruisers and the general public.' Other hints on cruising etiquette include 'don't hog the stall' in a public toilet and 'make sure you "fit in" with the place you are visiting;' in other words, if you don't look like you belong on a university campus, then don't queer the pitch for all the other queers who do. There is other, similar advice about how to blend in to a cruising environment (make sure you look 'blue collar' if you're heading to a working class environment), on the difference between discretion and recklessness (avoid parks in the winter when the bush cover is less dense), and the importance of cleaning up after you're done – all helpful hints for the freshman cruiser.[2]

There is no doubt that cruising is quite specifically linked to sex, in a way that I have not always been suggesting in *Backward Glances*. Indeed CFS is sponsored by Bedfellow who make and distribute porn and the site is covered with photos of erect penises and images of men having all kinds of sex, and every click of the mouse elicits a pop-up window selling Bedfellow services. Keith encourages users to support the sponsor, in order to keep the services of CFS free for all. Whatever other functions the site might fulfil, men ejaculating, either with others or alone, in a toilet or at home, is clearly to the fore.

As I have been emphasizing, cruising the city of modernity at the end of the nineteenth century offered a way of moving through and experiencing the city and its crowds that, on the one hand, exploited the ambiguities and uncertainties of men on the streets and, on the other, enabled a kind of contact through a reciprocal encounter, an ideal connection (if you're Whitman). While searching for sex with other men has always been a significant element of cruising, it isn't necessarily its reason for being and, as Samuel Delaney indicates, many forms of social interaction occur in cruising, of which sex is just one. It is not necessarily the case, even now with multiple partners seemingly so much easier to acquire, that the kinds of chance encounters that occur in our cities or on the web always lead to sex, however much the initial encounter, whether real or virtual, may be erotically circumscribed in the mind. Web exchanges may serve a wide variety of purposes in people's lives, among which sex is only one, however significant.

If you go through the personals or the message board or the sex listings on CFS, it becomes clear pretty quickly that cruising is not an urban phenomenon. And, of course, it never was *only* an urban way of being. Although for my purposes cruising may have arisen out of the modern city, with its public spaces available for multiple uses and its anonymous multitude, it is certainly no longer a specifically urban contact. The CFS sex listings – which rely on users reporting on cruising sites, and so are only as reliable as its users – are global (although they concentrate on English-language countries, in particular the USA, the UK and Australia), and by typing in a particular region, users can learn what public areas or adult bookshops are good for meeting men near you. So, for example, if you happen to be interested in the Scottish Borders, you will learn that the A1 layby near Berwick is a good place to meet men on their own and also male/female couples looking for a third. Or if you happen to be in Almagordo, New Mexico, there is the Foothills Park in the afternoon; near Yokuska, Japan, American sailors hang out in the Naval Recreation Center's fifth-floor toilets. Where cruisers have found difficulty with police or queerbashers or thieves, warnings are noted, and some sites are given the 'Head's Up' signal indicating danger of one kind or another. With sites like CFS, cruising couldn't be made simpler, it seems, anywhere and always.

Although it isn't exclusively an urban form of contact, perhaps predictably, there are more sex listings in cities (whether in Chile or China), including 'street cruising', in addition to action in parks, bathhouses and bookstores. But the city is present not just as an organizing geographical principle locating cruisers and cruising grounds, the idea of the city encounter emerges as a familiar imaginative presence that finds its way on to the website in other ways, and echoes some the encounters I have discussed in chapters above. The correspondents' columns, for example, offer semi-regular reports on cruising in London, Vancouver, Seattle and New York, often in the form of brief reports on the cruising scene, or walking tours around the cruising grounds of the city. The Vancouver correspondent, Doug (now the 'Guidance Counselor' advice columnist) used to write lively, wry reports about the cruising scene in his city. In his March 2002 correspondence, 'Tea Room Musings', Doug writes:

> I remember 'back in the day' when I had just come out I bought my first Damron guidebook. As well as the listings for bars, baths, etc, there were numerous listings for 'tea rooms'. I didn't have a clue what that meant. When I eventually learned that this was the code for a public toilet that was cruisy I was a bit baffled. How could you do it there I wondered . . . both technically and psychologically?

And so he goes on to recount an encounter with four men in a toilet on the university campus where he once worked:

> We were four men connected without a word passing between us. I was totally turned on, and absolutely terrified. If someone was to walk in there was no chance we could pull ourselves together to avoid being caught. Quickly we both

came, and I left on weak legs. Walking away I had to wonder
... how could something like that happen? It was surreal to be
locked in passion, when just outside the unlocked door the
rest of the world was going about its business, shopping for
groceries. Time seems to stop and the outside world to fade
away, as you indulge yourself in please [sic] with no strings
attached. It's just so hot!

I'm sure that this is a quintessentially gay experience. There
is no way straight people are doing things like this. It's one of
the unique things that only gay men can really understand,
and therefore something for us to celebrate. So get out there
and find a cruisy toilet and revel in it.[3]

Here, Doug attempts to describe the perverse pleasure to be
derived from the moment of having sex in a public place, with
the risk of getting caught that that involves. On the one hand, he
is speaking nostalgically and knowingly to experienced cruisers,
taking others to a time 'back in the day' when they, too, didn't
know about tea rooms; on the other, he is addressing less experienced cruisers for whom the questions he asks are real, even
pressing. Interestingly, he believes tea room encounters are quintessentially defining experiences of what it means to be gay, but
that may be wishful thinking: not all gay men accept cruising as
a valid form of interaction and not all cruisers identify as gay.
Doug's columns are often formulaic in the sense that his content
is in part a sex guide (telling you that the toilet where this
encounter took place is still active), part autobiographical (you
learn about Doug across the columns, where he lives, what kind
of sex he enjoys, etc.), and part pornographic tale. Like nearly all
his columns, 'Tea Room Musings' has its own pornographic trajectory as a true story that describes the sex in graphic detail.
Other of Doug's columns ('The Wall' and 'Cheap Sex in the
Morning') similarly resemble both an informational guide and a
pornographic sex tale. Are these true stories really true? I suppose
they are as true as the story of Mr Clive and Mr Page, which is
to say, very true, in their own way.

Other columnists use the conventions of *flâneur* journalism, wandering the streets noting the urban scenes and commenting on the surroundings, but with one eye on the lookout for a possible random encounter. The Provincetown, Massachusetts, correspondent, Frank Carroll, offers a short account of the streets of this queer beachtown in Cape Cod, which presumably merits its own column because it is one of the most popular queer resorts in America, with tens of thousands of men and women heading there between Memorial Day and Labor Day each summer. It also has a distinguished past and present as a queer artists' colony, extending from the days of Eugene O'Neill and the Provincetown Players to the present (Mark Doty lived there and writes about its dunes, for example). 'I've been writing a monthly column about sex in Provincetown and I haven't even mentioned what it's like just walking down the streets here,' Frank writes, and where there are streets, there will be cruising:

> There are a lot of men on the streets at all times so there will always be cruising going on. That goes without saying wherever and whenever there are lots of men who have sex with men in the same place. I hope you're not reading this hoping for tips on *how* to cruise the streets, 'cause I ain't got any and, frankly, I don't think I'm that good at it. I can tell you where and when, though.[4]

And with that little burst of honesty, he goes on to mention the bars in town and sand dunes by the sea, and places such as Spiritus Pizza and Commercial Street. CFS's London correspondent, Joe, also uses the urban walkabout to reveal the secrets of the city, as seen in his column, 'Walking':

> One of the things about being a Londoner is that you tend to live your life away from the postcard picture that all visitors want to enjoy while here. I suppose the same applies to anyone living in any major tourist destination.

I couldn't remember the last time I'd walked past Big Ben. In fact I think I hadn't been there after they'd finished rebuilding Westminster tube station, which is awesome in its own right. If you take the right exit you'd be excused to miss Big Ben, as you'll find yourself right at the foot of it. Just look up and synchronize your watch.

This particular day a work engagement had taken me to the area. This also meant that my working day finished earlier than usual, just before 5 pm.

I'd made no plans for the evening, and found myself walking towards Big Ben as it chimed, undecided about what to do next.

It was a lovely, albeit cold, evening, and thoughts of venturing into Soho for drinks in some crowded gay pub were quickly dispelled in favour of some outdoor exploration.

Walking down the Thames carries the same thrill as hearing Big Ben chime. I set off downstream on the north side, on what's known as the Embankment. I knew of a cottage there. A bit late for it to be open. Anyway, a notice on the door informed that it was closed for refurbishment and that the temporary toilets further down the road should be used instead.

Joe continues his walk to the new toilets, but there's no action there – 'I had a pee, which is something I also use toilets for, and moved on' – and then makes his way past the landmarks of central London along the Thames, including the London Eye, the South Bank Centre (cruisy cottages inside now closed due to vandalism), Waterloo Station (Pleasuredrome sauna on Alaska Street, nearby) and up to Tate Modern. Here, he abandons his sexual pursuit and takes pleasure merely in his surroundings:

I took it easy for the rest of my visit. If anything, and in all its magnitude, this is a relaxing place. I proceeded to check all toilets on all floors. All offered the same potential. However, that evening I chose to enjoy the company of Monet, Picasso, Warhol . . .[5]

Shame he didn't see one of Hockney's toilet graffiti paintings owned by the Tate. Joe's idle urban ramble combines the relaxed and detached pose of the classic *flâneur* (except that Joe reveals that he detests crowds, suggesting that he's more of a Dostoevskyan 'underground man' than a Baudelairean *flâneur*) with the more goal-oriented intentions of the modern-day sexual cruiser. In mapping his walk, he notices a toilet here, a new hotel there and makes passing comments about architecture, urban regeneration and the sexual possibilities along his tour. He combines a *flâneur*'s panoramic viewpoint with the observations of a particular kind of individual on the streets, the cruiser. Moving through the city is a motif in a later column, from November 2001, when Joe takes the opportunity of a day off work to venture out into parts of London hitherto unknown; in other words, he becomes an urban explorer:

> I went out exploring – visiting those venues I'd heard of or read about but which are so far out of the way that they only lend themselves to be visited on days like this. Can't remember the exact itinerary, not that you may be interested in it. Anyway, one of the good things about this particular leisure pursuit is that you get to see parts of town you wouldn't dream of visiting otherwise. At times this entails nice surprises ...

First he visits 'some cottage in some park', but not one he recommends, and then heads to the tube, which is urban-rumoured to be a great place to cruise:

> To be honest, I've been cruised on trains and train platforms. I'm even guilty of having sex with train staff on train company premises that then turned into romantic liaisons that turned sour. However, as a voyeur connoisseur I discovered that there's a different sort of fun in witnessing the cruising between others.
> It was about 7 pm and I was on the Central line noticing this plump, short office girl in a skirt that kept slipping up and

her dirty looks across to this suited guy who was transfixed by the saucy unsubtle performance of her hands, thighs and eyes. They both changed at the same station. I should've followed them to find out if indeed there exists a straight ritual equivalent to cruising. Ulterior conversations with straight friends have revealed that their dating and mating habits are not as far removed from those of the gay world as gay folklore would make us believe.

On this other occasion I was sitting one side seat away from this guy who kept alternating glances at me and the guy sitting opposite him. The guy opposite was carrying luggage and kept nodding off. I'd say he'd just flown in on long haul. Neither was my type, so I didn't clock in a description. They were both average gay guys. I was busy playing with my newly acquired MiniDisc player and excited about the prospect of my destination as to get distracted by occasional glances.

Being a voyeur, of course, Joe gets distracted by the glances of those two average gay men, just as he had been distracted by the straight couple. He continues to monitor the men's glancing, not least because one of them gets 'this massive hardon down the inside leg of his jeans'. In fact, Joe is so interested in their story that he names them as characters in his own – 'Mr Glancer' and 'Mr Opposite'. It turns out that Mr Glancer leaves his business card on Mr Opposite's thigh when he gets up to leave at his stop, which provokes Mr Opposite to leave the train and join him on the platform for a chat. 'I could've made an attempt to find out what would be next but by then the scene had become too commonplace', Joe reveals.[6] What attracts Joe's attention is the cruise, the exchange of glances, not what results from it, not the sexual encounter. And interestingly, according to Joe (and contrary to what Frank in Vancouver believes), cruising may not be the privilege of gay men – the kinds of silent contacts and secret codes Joe relishes are interpreted as ways of disrupting the commonplace, of queering the routines of everyday life. Thought about in that way, an 'office girl' and a 'suited man' can perhaps be as queer in their cruising as two gay men.

There are still other ways in which the city figures prominently in the conceptualization of cruising on CFS. A feature article put on line in 1997 (not written by a city correspondent) proposes the skateboarder as a new kind of urban cruiser, one whose sexuality is as fluid as the movements of his lithe body on the board, and one for whom skating is a 'lifestyle' not just a sport or fad, as the author Skateboy, a 24-year-old, attests:

> I've been skating since before it became a lifestyle. I've watched skating transform from a mode of transportation (I rode my board to school everyday for six years) to a competitive sport, and then to a complete lifestyle. I live amongst the skaters – I carry my board with me almost everywhere I go, and I know I've always got other guys to thrash with anytime I want to take the edge off. Sometimes, though, I need more than to just take the edge off, skating around a parking lot – I can rely on other skaters to release sexual tension, and so can anyone else who really gets into skaterboy like I do.

Skaterboy tells the reader how to dress to impress skaters, where to go to find them, and how to decide which ones to approach. Happily, lots of skaters do not resist the advances of cruising men because 'the majority of skaterboys do not suffer from any type of sexual identity crisis – they're usually hard-core, tough guys who are willing to try almost anything once'. While 'traditional cruising methods do not work with skaters' – for example, no foot tapping, crotch grabbing or have-you-got-a-light chat-up lines for them – it is helpful that

> skaters are into eye contact, and they often check each other out. A typical sure sign of interest is when a skater makes eye contact, checks you out, then makes eye contact again. The ritual usually starts from a ten to fifteen foot distance between

you, so you won't have much time to ponder. This scene calls for quick judgment, but it's nearly fool proof.[7]

The streets of the city are where the cruiser and skater overlap, and where the skater's unconventional thrasher 'lifestyle' and fluid sexual attitudes to gender and sexuality meet. In fact, the way the skateboarder moves through the city, appropriating public spaces and finding unplanned uses and meanings for architecture, suggests a resistance to the conventional understandings of the modern city similar to that of the urban cruiser.

As the city reports and other features suggest, there is clearly an Anglo-North American bias on the website. This may be for any number of reasons – having to do with language, access to technology and the culturally specific forms of cruising that may not 'translate' in all cultures other than as global sex tourism – but one of the things CFS and other sites push us to think about are the ways practices of urban modernity – such as city cruising – are imbricated in the so-called global village, the cybercity. To talk about global cybercruising at all is an odd thing. What cruising requires, as I have been discussing it so far, is a specific geography in which the encounter takes place, at least if it is a real meet. This can be a street, park, embankment, arcade, public toilet, corner – the sexual geography of the city has been crucial in the creation of cruising networks in the culture of Western cities. Passing down from generation to generation the knowledge of this geography (through oral culture, queer folklore if you like, and the various cultural productions of the city – literature, journalism, visual culture, etc.) has certainly been one way that cruising as an alternative urban practice has continued. As Nina Wakeford, writing about cyberqueer studies, suggests, 'cyberspaces . . . resist an orderly cartography', and the internet is a medium that challenges fundamentally the significance of conventional borders and boundaries, of concepts like the nation state itself.[8] If it is true that cyberspace enacts a form of global deterritorialization (one way of defining globalization), then what becomes of cruising, which seemingly requires a geographical specificity, if only to have something to transgress?

One answer may be that cybercruisers – and sites related to cruising – reimagine what 'space' is, although these sites also rely very much on conventional images, metaphors and representations of familiar spaces, as we have seen in the correspondents' columns. Or, to take another example, cruising chat rooms are frequently not so much about crossing and remapping boundaries and establishing geography (defining spaces, like 'rooms') and locating individuals – they are organized in order to place you in relation to a room full of others. So in the men's chatroom in *gaydar.co.uk* for the UK, the first rooms you can enter are London-based chatrooms: London 1, 2, 3, 4, 5; then London South 1 and 2; etc. After London, the rest of the UK is geographically carved up – by county and by metropolitan centre – and after all these geographical locations, we come to the 'theme' rooms catering for sexual tastes and fetishes (sports kit, wrestling, students, leather, etc.). The rest of the world, or what *appears* to be the rest of the world, is similarly carved up according to geography. (This pattern is one that is repeated in the other *gaydar* sites, in the USA, France, Argentina, Portugal, Spain, Mexico and Italy, for example.)

Within the rooms, geography is equally important, often demarcated by profile names that serve to locate the user. So, for example, in the London East 1 room, you will find profile names such as AndrewEETCR (indicating the Easy Everything internet café located on Tottenham Court Road in central London); SE13Tom25 (presumably a 25-year-old guy named Tom located in that postcode); E13lukin4fun121 (someone in east London, not looking for group sex); NW2Horny (someone in north London), NoStringsE3 (east London, in Bow), MileBender (a gay guy in Mile End, east London); E2usa (an American in Bethnal Green). Streets, neighbourhoods, postcodes – all are significant ways of representing yourself in chatrooms, and all re-establish borders, boundaries and conventional notions of location. This isn't the only way of presenting yourself, but it is one of the most common, and often when a profile name chooses to focus on a kind of social marker other than geography ('LondonIrish', say, or 'Thickcut', 'Student19', 'MarriedBiGuy'), some indication of location is offered in the tag line that accompanies the profile name on screen. It may be that specific locations are used by those who are most serious about meeting up for a 'real' meet, but that may not necessarily be so. Location may only matter if the virtual chat becomes actual – that is, if the cybercruise turns into a sexual meet – at which point hitting the streets of the city becomes necessary once more. So while the conceptualization of the spaces of cyberspace is layered – so that an interior space (the room) contains external space (London East) – conventional mappings of space and place are recognizable and important to one of the functions of the chatroom.

There is an argument that what cyberqueer spaces such as CFS and other sites create are new places where virtual communities are created, and evidence of these new communities abounds. Youth around the world is served by websites such as the Australian-based *mogenic.com*, which describes itself as being:

> a special place on the net where gay and lesbian youth have the freedom to exchange ideas, share experiences, discuss coming out, make friends, read interesting content and most importantly: *make contact*.
>
> Literally millions of young people around the world are making Mogenic a daily ritual. We are seeking your support to develop and for Mogenic to cater to the overwhelming demand for increased services.
>
> We incite you to help Mogenic help gay, lesbian, bisexual and transgender youth (GLBT) know that they are not alone, that there is a community of acceptance, vibrancy, support, beauty and pride. A community that cares for the positive advancement of its young people – *like any community should*.[9]

On a different gay youth website, *youth.org*, Leroy Aarons, arguing against overregulating access to the internet for teenagers, similarly suggests that it is through the web that new kinds of social formations can occur:

> I'm especially worried when I think of tens of thousands of gay kids who live isolated, invisible lives, bereft of contact with another gay teen or with anyone, for that matter, to whom they can talk. For an increasing number of gay and lesbian youngsters, on-line communication is a magic carpet that lifts them beyond their stifling geographic and psychological boundaries to a land of conversation, information and potentially life-saving interaction.[10]

As Aarons indicates, it is partially through spatial reconfiguration and deterritorialization in a globally networked world that new communities can be imagined. On the internet, there is no centre, and consequently no periphery – there are clusters of space – an amorphous constellation of connections that we tend to map using routine geographies but which can only ever be tentative and certainly not static because they are frequently shifting. On CFS, the world of cruising is continually being remapped by its user-cruisers. In this seemingly wide open cyberspace, the idea of marginal communities and subculture seems no longer relevant in the ways we have tended to understand those terms, and, as *mogenic.com* can rightly claim, new communities and new contacts can be forged. Cultural pluralism abounds now – whole new groups of global communities are formed, and a world of difference in the public sphere of the internet is created. Fredric Jameson suggests that in thinking of globalization in these cultural terms,

> you will slowly emerge into a postmodern celebration of difference and differentiation. Suddenly all the cultures around the world are placed in tolerant contact with each other in a kind of immense cultural pluralism which it would be very difficult not to welcome. Beyond that, beyond the dawning celebration of cultural difference, and often very closely linked

to it, is a celebration of the emergence of a whole immense range of groups, races, genders, ethnicities, into the speech of the public sphere . . .[11]

But we cannot take these new emerging communities *as communities* for granted, and it is always worth reminding ourselves that these communities can be as exclusive in their way as many other kinds. It might be worth asking, for example, whether for all its virtues, a site like *mogenic.com* perpetuates a particular kind of discussion of GLBT life that in fact has little or nothing to say to many non-English-speaking cultures. Or if we push the idea of community to include something like a global community of cruisers through sites like CFS, are we actually eliding the differences between, say, gloryhole etiquette in Belfast and cruising in Bombay, Beijing or Bangkok? Perhaps cruising is the same the world over, but perhaps it isn't and there is no reason we should assume that it is. Whether through the accumulation of websites like CFS and the standardization of chatroom formats, such a thing as a homogeneous global cruising practice that transcends cultural specificity will emerge is a matter of question. Whether or not it is a good thing, a matter of opinion. I think it probably is not. In fact, the whole notion of a community of cruisers seems to me to be completely at odds with the dissident potential (still) of the individual cruiser.

Often, what gets lost in the cybercruising of the twentieth century, among other things, is real contact. Cruising, as idealists like Whitman imagined it, enabled connections between two people that seemed to exist apart from or in resistance to isolating tendencies of modernity. Today, the cruiser seems to me to be in danger of being as alienated as everyone else – isolated behind a computer screen, alone in a room or in the collective (communal?) isolation of an internet café, chatting. What has been lost, arguably, is the significance of the fleeting moment of reciprocal gaze, that backward glance, in which the possibility of a sudden radical alternative might be realized for the everyday man in the street.

References

Chapter One: Ambiguous Cities

1 See Tom Conley, "*'Le Cineaste de la vie moderne'*: Paris as a Map in Film, 1924–34' in *Parisian Fields*, ed. Michael Sherringham (London, 1996), esp. pp. 71–2, and on Baudelaire and memory see Richard Terdiman, *Present Past: Modernity and the Memory Crisis* (Ithaca and London, 1993), pp. 109–10.

2 Charles Baudelaire, *The Flowers of Evil*, trans. James McGowan (Oxford and New York, 1993), pp. 173–7.

3 Marshall Berman, *All That Is Solid Melts Into Air: The Experience of Modernity* (New York and London, 1982), p. 133.

4 Baudelaire, *Flowers of Evil*, pp. 177–81.

5 Ibid., pp. 181–7.

6 Charles Baudelaire, *The Prose Poems and La Fanfarlo*, trans. Rosemary Lloyd (Oxford and New York, 1991), p. 44.

7 Charles Baudelaire, *Selected Writings on Art and Literature*, trans. P. E. Charvet (London, 1992), p. 399.

8 Ibid., p. 402.

9 Ibid., p. 403.

10 In *Present Past*, writing about Baudelaire, Richard Terdiman says that modernity is 'a reflex of ambivalence in the face of the transformations of the world', p. 132.

11 James Abbott McNeill Whistler, *The Gentle Art of Making Enemies* (New York, 1967), p. 143.

12 Ibid., p. 144.

13 See Denys Sutton, *The Art of James McNeill Whistler* (London, 1963), p. 68.

14 Baudelaire, *Selected Writings*, p. 401.

15 Quoted in Rosemary Lloyd, *Baudelaire's World* (Ithaca and London, 2002), pp. 153–4. See Charles Baudelaire, *Oeuvres Completes* (Paris, 1968), pp. 544–5.

16 See Denys Sutton, *James McNeill Whistler: Paintings, Etchings, Pastels and Watercolours* (London, 1966), p. 23.

17 Charles Dickens, *Dombey and Son*, ed. Valerie Purton (London, 1997), p. 63 and p. 213.

18 Charles Dickens, *Our Mutual Friend*, ed. Stephen Gill (London, 1971), p. 479.

19 Lynda Nead, *Victorian Babylon: People, Streets and Images in Nineteenth-Century London* (New Haven and London, 2000), p. 4.

20 See, for example, Deborah Nord, *Walking the Victorian Streets: Women, Representation, and the City* (Ithaca and London, 1995), chapter 7.

21 Walt Whitman, *Leaves of Grass*, ed. Jerome Loving (Oxford and New York, 1990), pp. 68–9.

22 Baudelaire, *Selected Writings*, pp. 400–01.

23 Edgar Allan Poe, 'The Man of the Crowd,' in *Collected Works of Edgar Allan Poe, II: Tales and Sketches, 1831–1842*, ed. Thomas Ollive Mabbott (Cambridge, MA, and London, 1978), pp. 510–11.

24 Walter Benjamin, *Charles Baudelaire: A Lyric Poet in the Era of High Capitalism*, trans. Harry Zohn (London and New York, 1997), p. 37.

25 Ibid., pp. 40–41.

26 Ibid., p. 55.

27 Janet Wolff, 'The Invisible *Flâneuse*: Women and the Literature of Modernity', *Theory, Culture and Society*, II/3 (1985), p. 41.

28 See also Elizabeth Wilson, 'The Invisible *Flâneur*', *New Left Review*, 195 (September–October 1992), pp. 90–110.

29 Nord, *Walking the Victorian Streets*, p. 12.

30 See Janet Wolff, 'The Artist and *Flâneur*: Rodin, Rilke and Gwen John in Paris', in *The Flâneur*, ed. Keith Tester (London and New York, 1994), esp. pp. 124–6.

31 Sally R. Munt, *Heroic Desire: Lesbian Identity and Cultural Space* (London and Washington, DC, 1998), chapter 2.

32 Dana Arnold, *Re-presenting the Metropolis: Architecture, Urban Experience and Social Life in London 1800–1840* (Aldershot, 2000), pp. 26–7.

33 Deborah Parsons, '*Flâneur* or *Flâneuse*? Mythologies of Modernity', *New Formations*, 38 (Summer 1999), pp. 91–100. For a more extended discussion of these issues, see Parsons's book, *Streetwalking the Metropolis: Women, the City and Modernity* (Oxford and New York, 2000).

34 Ibid., p. 96.

35 Baudelaire, *The Flowers of Evil*, p. 189.

36 Michel de Certeau, *The Practice of Everyday Life*, trans. Steven Rendall (Berkeley, CA, 1988), p. 117.

37 Ibid., p. 93.

38 Walter Benjamin, *Arcades Project*, trans. Howard Eiland and Kevin McLaughlin (Cambridge, MA, and London, 1999), p. ix. Simon Gunn describes Benjamin's project as one 'based on the idea of montage – hence the assemblage of fragments of theory and concrete historical detail, quotation and interpretation, arranged on a principle of dis/association', in 'City of Mirrors: *The Arcades Project* and Urban History', *Journal of Victorian Culture*, VII/2 (Autumn 2002), p. 265.

39 Ibid., p. 10.

40 Ibid., [J47,5], [J47,6], [J47a,1], p. 314.

41 Ibid., [M16a,2], [M16a,3], [M16a,4], p. 447.

42 Gunn, 'City of Mirrors,' p. 266. See also Scott McCraken, 'Random Patterns, Flashes of Insight: Walter Benjamin's *Arcades Project*', *Journal of Victorian Culture*, VII/2 (Autumn 2002), who writes that 'traces of the forgotten or only dimly remembered dream are to be found in the most transitory elements of modernity. In fact, the more transitory, the more likely they

are to evoke that which has been lost to consciousness,' p. 281.
43 Susan Buck–Morss, *The Dialectics of Seeing: Walter Benjamin and the Arcades Project* (London, 1989), p. x.
44 See Gunn, 'City of Mirrors,' p. 267.
45 Benjamin, *Arcades Project*, [J72,5], p. 356.

Chapter Two: Cruising Modernity

1 For recent conceptual discussions of writing the history of homosexuality, see David M. Halperin, *How To Do The History of Homosexuality* (Chicago and London, 2002); Lisa Duggan provides a lucid account of 1990s queer politics in 'Making It Perfectly Queer', in *Sex Wars: Sexual Dissent and Political Culture*, ed. Lisa Duggan and Nan D. Hunter (New York and London, 1995), pp. 155–72; Alan Sinfield discusses identity categories in 'Lesbian and Gay Taxonomies', *Critical Inquiry*, XXIX/1 (Autumn 2002).
2 John Howard, *Men Like That: A Southern Queer History* (Chicago and London, 1999), p. 6.
3 For a different but very suggestive reading of Benjamin's relevance to queer considerations, see Dianne Chisholm, 'A Queer Return to Walter Benjamin', *Journal of Urban History*, XXIX/1 (November 2002), pp. 25–38.
4 Neil Bartlett, *Who Was That Man? A Present for Mr Oscar Wilde* (London, 1988), p. xx and p. xxi.
5 Scott Bravmann, *Queer Fictions of the Past: History, Culture, and Difference* (Cambridge, 1997), p. 97.
6 Jeffrey Weeks, *Making Sexual History* (Cambridge, 2000), p. 3.
7 Anonymous, *Sins of the Cities of the Plain or the Reflections of a Mary Ann* (London and New York, 1881) p. 79.
8 See Morris B. Kaplan, 'Who's Afraid of John Saul? Urban Culture and the Politics of Desire in Late Victorian London', *GLQ*, V/3, who suggests that the opening to *Sins* 'is a plausible rendering of the practices and fantasies of gay cruising in a London setting, where similar, though less discreet, encounters may still be observed today', p. 284.
9 William A. Cohen, *Sex Scandal: The Private Parts of Victorian Fiction* (Durham, NC, and London, 1996), p. 124.
10 Judith Walkowitz, *City of Dreadful Delight: Narratives of Sexual Danger in Late-Victorian London* (London, 1992), p. 50 and pp. 128–30.
11 Bartlett, *Who Was That Man?*, p. 253.
12 Derek Jarman, *At Your Own Risk: A Saint's Testament*, ed. Michael Christie (New York, 1993), p. 55.
13 *The Times* (9 February 1876), p. 11.
14 See Walkowitz, *City of Dreadful Delight*, esp. chapters 2–4.
15 See Eve Sedgwick, *Between Men: English Literature and Male Homosocial Desire* (New York, 1985), chapter 9.
16 Robert Louis Stevenson, *Dr Jekyll and Mr Hyde and Other Stories* (Harmondsworth, 1979), p. 31. On the queer content of *Dr Jekyll and Mr Hyde*, see Elaine Showalter, *Sexual Anarchy: Gender and Culture at the 'fin de siècle'* (New York, 1990), pp. 111–14.
17 Stevenson, *Dr Jekyll and Mr Hyde*, p. 33.

18 Oscar Wilde, *The Picture of Dorian Gray*, ed. Peter Ackroyd (1891; London, 1985), p.73.

19 Charles Silverstein and Edmund White, *The Joy of Gay Sex* (New York, 1977), pp. 74–5.

20 Quoted in R. Bruce Brasell, '*My Hustler:* Gay Spectatorship as Cruising', *Wide Angle*, XIV/2 (April 1992), p. 60.

21 Jonathan Crary, *Techniques of the Observer: On Vision and Modernity in the Nineteenth Century* (Cambridge and London, 1990), pp. 10–11.

22 Ibid., p. 21.

23 Georg Simmel, 'The Metropolis and Mental Life', in *On Individuality and Social Forms*, ed. Donald N. Levine (Chicago and London, 1971), p. 325.

24 Ibid., p. 324.

25 George Simmel, 'Sociology of the Senses' in *Simmel on Culture: Selected Writings*, ed. David Frisby and Mike Featherstone (London, 1997), pp. 111–12.

26 Henning Bech, *When Men Meet: Homosexuality and Modernity*, trans. Teresa Mesquit and Tim Davies (Chicago, 1997), p. 118.

27 Ibid., p. 106.

28 Ibid., p. 106.

29 Roland Barthes, *Incidents*, trans. Richard Howard (Berkeley, Los Angeles and Oxford, 1992), p. 59.

30 Edmund White, *The Flâneur: A Stroll Through the Paradoxes of Paris* (London, 2001), p. 145.

31 See Priscilla Parkhurst Ferguson, 'The *flâneur* on and off the streets of Paris', in *The Flâneur*, ed. Keith Tester (London and New York, 1994), pp. 22–42.

32 *The Beginner's Guide to Cruising* (Washington, DC, 1964), p. 1.

Chapter Three: London: Mysteries of the Passers-by

1 'More "Mysteries"', *The Times* (10 July 1876), p. 9. See also 'The Jermyn-Street Mysteries', *The Times* (12 July 1876), p. 12.

2 Jermyn Street runs parallel to Piccadilly on the south, and runs from St James's Street on the west, crossing Lower Regent Street on the east.

3 Anthony Trollope, 'The Turkish Bath', *Saint Paul's Magazine*, V (October 1869), 110.

4 C. Bartholomew, *The Turkish Bath in Convalescence* (London, 1869). On Victorian Turkish Baths generally, see the following: C. Bartholomew, *The Turkish Bath* (London, 1869); John Le Gay Brereton, MD, 'A Lecture on the Action and Uses of the Turkish Bath', (London, 1869); E. Wilson, *Eastern, or Turkish Bath* (London, 1861); R. Owen Allsop, *The Turkish Bath: Its Design and Construction* (London, 1890). Malcolm Shifrin has created a helpful website on Victorian baths, see www.victorianturkishbath.org.

5 *The Times*, 28 February 1862, p. 10.

6 Wilson, *Eastern, or Turkish Bath*, p. 36.

7 Trollope, 'The Turkish Bath,' p. 111.

8 Ibid., p. 114.

9 See Mark W. Turner, *Trollope and the Magazines: Gendered Issues in Mid-Victorian Britain* (Basingstoke, 2000), pp. 201–7.

10 It is worth considering the Jermyn Street baths alongside twentieth-century gay bathhouses. For interpretations of twentieth-century baths, see in particular: Ira Tattelman, 'Speaking to the Gay Bathhouse: Communicating in Sexually Charged Spaces', in *Public Sex/Gay Space*, ed. William L. Leap (New York, 1999), pp. 71–94; Aaron Betsky, *Queer Space: Architecture and Same-Sex Desire* (New York, 1997), chapter 4; Ira Tattelman, 'Presenting a Queer (Bath)House', in *Queer Frontiers: Millennial Geographies, Genders, and Generations*, ed. Joseph Boone, Martin Dupuis, Karin Quimby, Cindy Savner, Debra Silverman and Rosemary Weatherston (Madison, WI, 2000), pp. 222–58.

11 Denys Forrest, *Foursome in St James: The Story of the East India, Devonshire, Sports and Public Schools Club* (London, 1982), p. 9.

12 Charles Lethbridge Kingsford, *The Early History of Piccadilly, Leicester Square, Soho and Their Neighbourhood* (Cambridge, 1925), p. 97.

13 Joan Glasheen, *St James's, London* (Chichester, Sussex, 1987), p. 30.

14 James Gardiner, *Who's a Pretty Boy Then? One Hundred Years of Gay Life in Pictures* (London, 1996), p. 24.

15 Thanks to Matt Houlbrook who first suggested this to me.

16 Derek Jarman, *At Your Own Risk: A Saint's Testament*, ed. Michael Christie (New York, 1992), p. 12.

17 See Matt Houlbrook's discussion of the queer geography of London in 'For Whose Convenience? Gay Guides, Cognitive Maps and the Construction of Homosexual London 1917–1967', in *Identities in Space: Contested Terrains in the Western City since 1850*, ed. Simon Gunn and Robert J. Morris (Aldershot, 2001), esp. p. 173.

18 Michael Hill, *Tragedy in Jermyn Street: A Play* (London, 1934), p. 8. Alan Sinfield briefly discusses the play in *Out on Stage: Lesbian and Gay Theatre in the Twentieth Century* (New Haven and London, 1999), pp. 122–3.

19 Neil Bartlett, *Mr Clive and Mr Page* (London, 1996), pp. 27–8.

20 Ibid., 30.

21 Bartlett quotes an account of this in *Mr Clive and Mr Page*, p. 195. Unlike many of the extracts 'quoted' in the novel, this one is real.

22 Ibid., p. 1.

23 Ibid., p. 50.

24 Letter from Neil Bartlett to the author, January 5, 2003.

25 'What the "Yellow Book" is to be', *The Sketch*, v (11 April 1894), p. 558.

26 Anna Gruetzner Robins... [[AQ details?]]1992, p. 16.

27 Lisa Tickner, *Modern Life and Modern Subjects: British Art in the Early Twentieth Century* (New Haven and London, 2000), p. 12.

28 John Felstiner, *The Lies of Art: Max Beerbohm's Parody and Caricature* (London, 1973), pp. 9–10.

29 Charles Baudelaire, *Selected Writings on Art and Literature*, trans. P. E. Charvet (London, 1992), p. 427.

30 Max Beerbohm, 'A Defence of Cosmetics,' *Yellow Book*, I (April 1894), p. 65 and p. 67.

31 Richard Le Gallienne, *The Romantic '90s* (London, 1993), p. 122.

32 Karl Beckson, *London in the 1890s: A Cultural History* (London and New York, 1992), suggests that 'the city became for writers of the decade, as it had not

been for the mid–Victorians, the symbol of one's soul with implications of spiritual and psychological turmoil', p. 266.

33 Charlotte Mew, 'Passed', *Yellow Book*, II (July 1894), p. 126.

34 Ibid., p. 130 and p. 136.

35 Ibid., p. 139.

36 Henry Harland, 'When I Am King,' *Yellow Book*, III (October 1894), p. 71.

37 Ibid., p. 72.

38 John Davidson, 'Thirty Bob a Week', *Yellow Book*, II (July 1894), p. 99.

39 George Egerton, 'A Lost Masterpiece: A City Mood, Aug. '93,' *Yellow Book*, I (April 1894), p. 189.

40 Ibid., p. 190 and p. 191.

41 Henry Harland, 'A Responsibility', *Yellow Book*, II (July 1894), pp. 104–5.

42 Ibid., p. 105.

43 Ibid., pp. 105–6.

44 Mew, 'Passed', p. 126.

45 Harland, 'A Responsibility,' pp. 111–12.

46 Ibid., p. 115.

Chapter Four: New York: City of Orgies, Walks and Joys

1 The only monograph on Gedney is *What Was True: The Photographs and Notebooks of William Gedney,* ed. Margaret Sartor and Geoff Dyer (New York and London, 2000).

2 Ibid., p. 17.

3 Ibid., p. 17 and p. 18.

4 Quoted in ibid., p. 39.

5 See the profile of Klein by John Heilpern, in *William Klein, Photographs* (New York, 1981), p. 13.

6 Walt Whitman, 'Ourselves and the *Eagle*', *Brooklyn Daily Eagle*, 1 June 1846, quoted in *The Uncollected Poetry and Prose of Walt Whitman*, ed. Emory Holloway (London, 1922), p. 115.

7 Geoff Dyer, 'A Long Patience,' in Sartor and Dyer, *What Was True*, pp. 174–75.

8 Walt Whitman, 'Democratic Vistas', *Specimen Days and Collect* (Philadelphia, 1883), p. 211.

9 Ibid., p. 203.

10 Walt Whitman, *Notebooks and Unpublished Prose Manuscripts*, ed. Edward F. Grier, IV (New York, 1984), p. 1326.

11 Ibid., pp. 246–62.

12 Whitman, *Notebooks and Unpublished Prose Manuscripts*, I, p. xiv.

13 See Charles Shively, *Calamus Lovers: Walt Whitman's Working Class Camerados* (San Francisco, 1987), chapter 3, esp. pp. 54–62.

14 Richard Maurice Bucke, ed., *Calamus: A Series of Letters Written During the Years 1868–1880 By Walt Whitman to a Young Friend (Peter Doyle)* (Boston, 1897), p. 23.

15 Gary Schmidgall, *Walt Whitman: A Gay Life* (New York, 1998), p. xxvix and p. xxviii.

16 J. A. Symonds to Walt Whitman, 3 August 1890, in *The Letters of John*

Addington Symonds, ed. Herbert M. Schueller and Robert L. Peters, III
(Detroit, 1969), p. 483.

17 Symonds to J. W. Wallace, 19 December 1892, in ibid., p. 792.

18 John Addington Symonds, *Walt Whitman: A Study* (London, 1893), p. 72.

19 Edward Carpenter, *Some Friends of Walt Whitman: A Study in Sex Psychology*,
Publication No. 13, The British Society for the Study of Sex Psychology
(London, 1924), p. 12 and pp. 14–15. See Eve Kosofky Sedgwick's interpreta-
tion of Whitman's English readers in *Between Men: English Literature and Male
Homosocial Desire* (New York, 1985), 'Coda'.

20 Xavier Mayne, *The Intersexes: A History of Semisexualism as a Problem of Social
Life* (privately printed, 1908).

21 Walt Whitman, 'Subject – Poem: The Two Vaults', in *Uncollected Poetry and
Prose of Walt Whitman*, II, p. 92.

22 Horace Traubel, *Walt Whitman in Camden*, I (1908; reprinted New York,
1961), p. 417. On Bohemian New York and Pfaff's, see Albert Parry, *Garrets
and Pretenders* (New York, 1933).

23 Christine Stansell, 'Whitman at Pfaff's: Commercial Culture, Literary Life
and New York Bohemia at Mid–Century', *Walt Whitman Quarterly*, X/3
(Winter 1993), p. 107.

24 Walt Whitman, *Leaves of Grass*, ed. Jerome Loving (New York and Oxford,
1990), 'A Broadway Pageant', p. 194.

25 Ibid., p. 193.

26 Ibid., 'To You,' p. 18.

27 Ibid., 'To a Stranger,' p. 106.

28 Ibid., 'City of Orgies,' p. 105.

29 Ibid., 'Among the Multitude,' p. 111.

30 Dana Brand, *The Spectator and the City in Nineteenth-Century American
Literature* (Cambridge, 1991), p. 11 and p. 12.

31 See ibid., p. 177.

32 Ibid., p. 183.

33 Whitman, 'A Glimpse', *Leaves of Grass*, p. 109.

34 Other critics have written helpfully and thoughtfully about Whitman's
cruising. Michael Warner finds a 'phenomenology of cruising' in Whitman.
See Michael Warner, 'Whitman Drunk', in *Breaking the Bounds: Walt Whitman
and American Cultural Studies*, ed. Betsy Erkkila and Jay Grossman (New York
and Oxford, 1996), p. 41. Alan Trachtenberg believes that 'Whitman cruises
the city in search of significant others – as [William] James will put it, "the
significance of alien lives" – and finds "You" in every encounter.' For
Trachtenberg, Whitman's cruising is a way of breaking down the barrier
between self and other, so that the two fuse together into a new identity, one
that offers the self up to another, one that does not necessarily cling to the
flâneur's power of detached objectification. See Alan Trachtenberg, 'Whitman's
Lesson of the City', in Erkkila and Grossman, *Breaking the Bounds*, p. 164.

35 David S. Reynolds, *Walt Whitman's America: A Cultural Biography* (New York,
1995), pp. 103–7.

36 George Chauncey, *Gay New York: Gender, Urban Culture, and the Making of the
Gay Male World, 1890–1940* (New York, 1994), chapter 1, especially pp. 33–7.

37 Jonathan Katz, *Gay American History* (New York, 1976), p. 52.

38 Earl Lind ('Ralph Werther' – 'Jennie June'), *Autobiography of an Androgyne* (New York, 1918, reprinted 1975), Appendix III.

39 Ibid., p. 110.

40 Ibid., p. 47.

41 Michael Bronski, ed., 'Introduction', *Pulp Friction* (New York, 2003), p. 8.

42 Edmund White, *The Farewell Symphony* (London, 1997), pp. 299–300. For a discussion of White's novel and promiscuity, see Ben Cove, *Cruising Culture: Promiscuity, Desire and American Gay Literature* (Edinburgh, 2000), pp. 180–86.

43 Renaud Camus, *Tricks: Twenty-Five Encounters*, trans. Richard Howard (New York and London, 1996), p. xiii.

44 Lind, *Autobiography*, pp. 59–60.

45 Ibid., p. 71.

46 Ibid, pp. 143–4.

47 Ibid., pp. 131–2.

48 Ibid., pp.134–5.

49 Ibid., p.145.

50 Robert K. Martin, '"City of Orgies"', in *Walt Whitman: An Encyclopaedia* (New York and London, 1998), p. 121. See also Martin's book *The Homosexual Tradition in American Poetry* (Austin, TX, 1979).

51 Quoted in Cove, *Cruising Culture*, p. 14.

Chapter Five: Backward Glances at Whitman

1 *The Times* (16 March 1954) p. 50.

2 Peter Wildeblood, *Against the Law* (London, 1955, reprinted 1999), p. 37.

3 Walt Whitman, *Notebooks and Unpublished Manuscripts*, ed. Edward F. Grier, II (New York, 1984), pp. 888–9. See also the editors' comments on p. 885 for a discussion of the decoding of these and similar passages.

4 Ibid., p. 889.

5 For accounts of Hockney's years at the Royal College of Art, see especially: Paul Melia, 'Showers, Pools and Power', in *David Hockney*, ed. Paul Melia (Manchester and New York, 1995), pp. 49–67; Alan Woods, 'Pictures Emphasizing Stillness', in *David Hockney*, ed. Melia, pp. 30–48; Peter Webb, *Portrait of David Hockney* (London, 1990); Paul Melia and Ulrich Luckhardt, *David Hockney: Paintings* (Munich and Pastel, 1994).

6 Wildeblood, *Against the Law*, p.34 and p. 35.

7 On this period, see Neil Miller, *Out of the Past: Gay and Lesbian History from 1869 to the Present* (London, 1995), pp. 282–6. See also Stephen Jeffery-Poulter, *Peers, Queers and Commons: The Struggle for Gay Law Reform, 1950–Present* (London, 1991) and Patrick Higgins, *Heterosexual Dictatorship: Male Homosexuality in Postwar Britain* (London, 1996).

8 Paul Melia, 'Showers, Pools and Power', p. 51.

9 David Hockney, *David Hockney by David Hockney: My Early Years*, ed. Nikos Stangos (London, 1976), pp. 62–3.

10 Jonathan Weinberg, *Speaking for Vice: Homosexuality in the Art of Charles Demuth, Marsden Hartley, and the First American Avant-Garde* (New Haven and London, 1993), p.133.

11 Michael Davidson, '"When the World Strips Down and Rouges Up"':

Redressing Whitman', in *Breaking the Bounds: Walt Whitman and American Cultural Studies*, ed. Betsy Erkkila and Jay Grossman (New York and Oxford, 1996), p. 226.

12 Allen Ginsberg, *Howl and Other Poems* (San Francisco, 1994), pp. 13–14.

13 For Ginsberg on Whitman, see the *Gay Sunshine Interview* with Ginsberg in *Spontaneous Mind: Selected Interviews 1958–1996*, ed. David Carter (London, 2001), esp. pp. 313–21.

14 Neil Bowers, 'The City Limits: Frank O'Hara's Poetry', in *Frank O'Hara: To Be True To A City*, ed. Jim Elledge (Ann Arbor, MI, 1990), p. 321.

15 Brad Gooch, *City Poet: The Life and Times of Frank O'Hara* (New York, 1993), p. 191. See also Davidson, '"When the World Strips…"', pp. 220–34. For a queer reading of O'Hara (although not in relation to Whitman), see David R. Jarraway, '"Vanilla Hemorrhages": The Queer Perversities of Frank O'Hara', *GLQ*, IV/1 (1998), pp. 67–108.

16 Frank O'Hara, 'Easter,' in *The Collected Poems of Frank O'Hara*, ed. Donald Allen (Berkeley, Los Angeles and London, 1995), p. 97.

17 See Gooch, *City Poet*, p. 197.

18 O'Hara, 'Homosexuality', in *The Collected Poems of Frank O'Hara*, p. 182.

19 Hockney, *David Hockney*, p. 44.

20 Derek Jarman, *At Your Own Risk: A Saint's Testament* (New York, 1993), p. 19.

21 For a discussion of these points, see Nancy Macdonald, *The Graffiti Subculture: Youth, Masculinity and Identity in London and New York* (Basingstoke, 2001), p. 158 and p. 203.

22 Samuel Delaney, *Times Square Red, Times Square Blue* (New York and London, 1999), pp. 123–4.

23 Ibid., pp. 56–7.

24 Whitman, 'We Two Boys Together Clinging', *Leaves of Grass*, ed. Jerome Loving (New York and Oxford, 1990), p. 108.

25 Hockney, *David Hockney*, p. 68.

26 Jarman, *At Your Own Risk*, p. 47.

27 David Wojnarowicz, *Close to the Knives: A Memoir of Disintegration* (London, 1992), p. 121.

28 See Woods, 'Pictures Emphasizing Stillness', p. 46; and Melia, 'Shower, Pools and Power', p. 53 and 57.

29 Andrew Causey, 'Mapping and Representing,' in *David Hockney*, ed. Paul Melia, p. 105.

30 Mark Doty, 'Letter to Walt Whitman', *Source* (London, 2002), p. 20.

31 Both 'Chance Meeting' and a couple of selections from *Salute, Walt Whitman* can be found in *The Essential Duane Michals*, ed. Marco Livingstone (Boston, New York et al., 1997).

Epilogue: Cruisingforsex

1 Cruisemaster, 'Welcome', http://www.cruisingforsex.com/firsttime.html, 8 May 2003.

2 Cruisemaster, 'Cruising 101: Skills for Safer, Successful Cruising', http://www.cruisingforsex.com/features/cruisingskills.html, 8 May 2003.

3 Doug, 'Tea Room Musings', http://www.cruisingforsex.com/correspondent/

VANCOUVER/doug6.html, 8 May 2003.

4 Frank Carroll, 'Street Smarts', http://www.cruisingforsex.com/
correspondentPTOWN/frank.html, 8 March 2001.

5 Joe, 'Walking',
http://www.cruisingforsex.com/correspondentLONDON/joe8.html, 3 March
2001

6 Joe, 'Train Travel on a Day', http://www.cruisingforsex.com/
correspondentLONDON/joe.html, 11 July 2001.

7 Skaterboy, 'Cruising for Sex on a Skateboard',
http://www.cruisingforsex.com/features/skaterboy.html, 9 May 2003.

8 Nina Wakeford, 'Cyberqueer,' in *Lesbian and Gay Studies: A Critical
Introduction*, ed. Andy Medhurst and Sally R. Munt (London and
Washington, DC, 1997), p. 22. See also Jon Stratton, 'Cyberspace and the
Globalization of Culture', in *Internet Culture* (New York and London, 1996).

9 'About Mogenic', http://www.mogenic.com/about/default.asp, 18 October
2001.

10 '*YAO Forum*: Porn on the Internet',
http://www.youth.org/yao/docs/porn.html, 18 October 2001.

11 Fredric Jameson, 'Notes on Globalization as a Philosophical Issue', in *The
Cultures of Globalization*, ed. Fredric Jameson and Masao Miyoshi (Durham,
NC, and London, 1998), pp. 57–7.

List of Illustrations

Acknowledgements

There are many people I would like to thank, but can't, because I never managed to catch their names, but they all helped a great deal in their way. Happily there are many other friends and colleagues whose names I do know, and who have also assisted me in a variety of ways, by offering advice, reading parts of the manuscript, suggesting leads and sharing ideas about cities and streets, swapping cruising stories, giving me a place to stay during research trips, and indulging me generally. In particular, Geoff Dyer, Richard Hornsey and Michael Slater provided me with materials I otherwise would not have found, and that have made aspects of the book more layered. In addition, I'd like to thank the following: Caterina Albano, Corin Bennett, Laurel Brake, Chiara Briganti, Tim Burton, Mark Campbell and Nick Manville, Joe Clement, Tim D'Arch Smith, Gavin Eddy, Carter Foster, Erik Friedly, Micaela Giebelhausen, Chris Goodhart and Les Hayden, John Howard, Richard Kaye, Caroline Levine, Jon McKenzie, Bob Mills, Nicole Pohl, Adrian Rifkin, Catherine Shearn, Ishtla Singh, John Stokes, Ann Thompson and Rebecca Wilson. As always, my parents have provided endless support in material and other ways, and I would like to thank them once again. Colleagues in the Department of English at King's College London and, before that, at University of Surrey Roehampton provided intellectually stimulating environments and material support which enabled the research for this book. I'd like to thank those postgraduates at King's in my 'Twentieth Century City' course in 2002 and in my 'Modernity and the City' course in 2003, whose intelligence and scepticism were provocative in equal measure. Brendan Murdock helped me in a number of ways but, in particular, I wish to thank him for his good humour, patience and loving support during the writing of this book.

The research for the book was undertaken at a number of institutions, to whose librarians and other staff I am grateful: London Metropolitan Archive; British Library; University of London Library; New York Public Library; Lesbian Herstory Archive; New York University Library. I would like to acknowledge the support of the British Academy for a travel grant that allowed me to visit collections in New York. Material from this book was presented to academic audiences at the University of Warwick, University of London, Manchester University, Kingston University, Carleton College, the London RSVP conference, the Philadelphia Northeast Victorian Studies Association conference, and the MLA conference in New York. For the use of visual material reproduced here I wish to thank Duke University, the London Metropolitan Archive, the British Library, the David Hockney Foundation, Tate Britain and Camden Council. Material that has been substantially revised first appeared as 'Cruising in Queer Street: Streetwalking Men in Late-Victorian London', in Kate Chedgzoy, Emma Francis and Murray Pratt, eds, *In a Queer Place: Sexuality and Belonging in British and European Contexts* (Aldershot, 2002), pp. 89–109.